Intarsia Artistry

12 Projects for Every Occasion

by Judy Gale Roberts and Jerry Booher

Fox Chapel Publishing Co., Inc.
1970 Broad Street
East Petersburg, PA 17520

© **1998, 2000 Fox Chapel Publishing**

Publisher: Alan Giagnocavo
Project Editor: Ayleen Stellhorn
Step-by-Step Photography: Jerry Booher
Gallery Photography: Bob Polett
Cover Photography: Bob Polett

ISBN # 1-56523-096-5

To order your copy of this book,
please send check or money order
for cover price plus shipping and handling (see back of book) to:
Fox Chapel Book Orders
1970 Broad Street
East Petersburg, PA 17520

Try your favorite book supplier first!

Manufactured in China

Table of Contents

Foreword

I have been creating Intarsia for about twenty years now. I still enjoy each project (some more than others) and eagerly await to finish the piece and hang it up for viewing. For me, working with the medium of wood is what has kept my interest all these years. I can make the same pattern twice and each time it will look different because of the wood. Then sanding and shaping the wood brings the piece to life. Occasionally the wood grain will inspire a pattern idea, other times I have different "prize" boards I think about using when I am designing patterns. A trip to the lumber yard is like going on a treasure hunt, sometimes there is a gold mine, other times nothing.

I cannot write much more without mentioning my partner, Jerry Booher. He has really fine-tuned the process. I have to admit he cuts the pieces out perfectly. He often says "you draw 'em, I'll saw 'em." (Well, he used to say it more than he does now.) He is also the one who looks over the pattern to make sure it is not too difficult to cut out and tries to edit the patterns before we offer them to everyone. I look at the design from more of an artist's view. He is able to look at it from the stand point of making the piece with the minimum of parts and ease in cutting those parts. Together we balance each other, I have learned to simplify many designs without compromising the composition. Initially when designing patterns, I had a tendency to have too many details, too many parts, which now I feel can be very distracting to the design.

This is our third Intarsia book and the second to focus on small projects. After the first book many of our long-time customers wrote and "came out of the closet." They commented that they had been reducing the larger patterns we sell since way back when. They found it easier and quicker to make the projects smaller. This works in most cases, but sometimes smaller is not always easier.

For the projects in this book, we used a scroll saw, however, they can be cut with a band saw as well. Some parts will need to be modified for a band saw, perhaps use a wood burner in place of some of the small "inside" cuts. There are 12 small Intarsia projects in this book. Each one can be used in a number of ways, from photo mat to applying them to wooden plates.

Wood selection and pattern usage are covered in the beginning of the book. Project One is a step-by-step demonstration of a simple Intarsia pattern to help get you started and teach you the basic skills involved in creating your own piece of Intarsia. Project Two is another step-by-step demonstration of a more complex pattern to show you many more skills that will help you in future projects. We feel that the step-by-step instructions on the two projects will teach you all the skills required to complete the other patterns in this book. Rather than go step-by-step on each project, we feel it is also important for your to learn how to go "solo" so to speak. Therefore, we have provided 10 additional projects for you to try. A pattern and notes are included for each to help you get started. After that, you're on your own. Remember, the whole technique is a learning process. Even after years of making Intarsia, I learn new things every day.

Wood Selection

Wood comes in a wide variety of colors and grain patterns. These eight wood samples show the color of the unfinished wood and the finished wood.

The above photo shows eight blocks of wood. We applied a clear finish to the lower half of each block to demonstrate how the wood will change color when a clear finish is applied. Notice that the white wood is least affected by the finish. In all cases, the finish does make the wood richer looking and brings out all the grain.

Most of the wood blocks pictured here are western red cedar. This wood is ideal for Intarsia and offers many variances in color. However, often I will have to use a different species of wood for the white color. The white wood pictured here is basswood. Basswood has its variances also and can be found in a very tan color to an almost pure white. For white wood I use either white pine, basswood or aspen.

The colors of the wood blocks pictured in Photo 1.1 are typical of the colors referred to in the Small

Intarsia projects. From left to right, the first block on the top row is considered "W," a white wood; the second is "L," a light shade of wood; the third is "M," a medium shade of wood; and the fourth is "ML," a medium-light shade of wood. The first block of wood on the lower row is "MD," a medium-dark shade of wood; the second is another "MD;" the third is "D," a dark shade of wood; and the final block on the lower row is also a "D," only darker than the previous block.

The darker shades of cedar are harder to find. I have better luck looking through the cedar fence picket pile. Even the 1" x 4" section may have more dark cedar than the 1" x 12" section. For these smaller Intarsia projects, the 1" x 6" fence pickets have ample width and provide an inexpensive wood to use.

I use the cedar because of the variety of colors and grain patterns produced by the tree. It is a soft wood, easy to work. Soft woods work well for wall-hung projects because they do not have to withstand the abuse furniture projects take. However, you still need to use care when handling cedar. It will scratch, ding and nick very easily. You may also use walnut (a dark wood), pecan (a medium color wood), maple or birch (light shades of wood) or any number of wood species. Any type of wood will work for Intarsia projects. The most important aspects are nice color and interesting grain patterns.

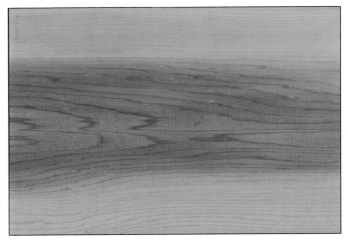

Though it is hard to find, red cedar sap wood can be used as white-colored wood in place of the more common basswood, pine or aspen.

Wood Selection

Sometimes with cedar I am able to find the sap wood, which is often very white. These areas are limited to about 2" wide, on average, on the outside edges of boards.

When choosing which boards to buy, I look for color first, then take a closer look to see what the grains are doing. I rarely buy the "knot-free" lumber. So many times you will find really unusual grain patterns around a knot. An intriguing part of Intarsia is choosing not only the color, but a grain pattern that can make a project come to life. Because we are working with many small parts, it is easy to work around the knots and other natural occurrences in the wood. Sometimes I will incorporate the knot into the project. Other times I remove the knot because it is so dark that it draws too much attention and distracts from the main subject matter.

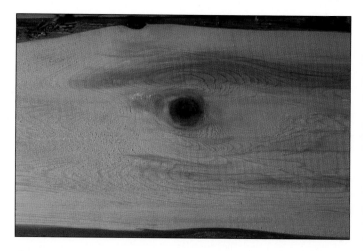

Streaks of color going through pieces of wood are perfect for creating sunsets and water.

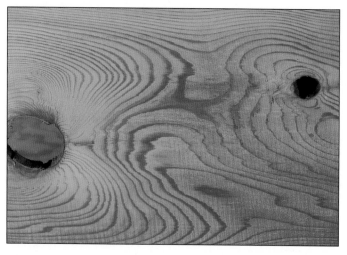

Knots in wood often force the grain of the wood to form interesting and unusual patterns that are beautiful when incorporated into Intarsia projects.

After working with grains I find myself studying wood everywhere and enjoying its natural beauty. Many interesting grain patterns are ideal for Intarsia. I look for wood that may have some streaks going through it. These boards make great sunsets, water, even rose petals. I stash prize boards waiting for just the right project. Sometimes the wood will inspire the pattern. I also buy straight-grained lumber. On each project I try to have a balance of straight grains and more unusual grains. Too many exotic grain patterns can get monotonous.

After making your wood selections, make sure the wood is dry. Often times the cedar is shipped wet. It is a good idea to let your wood dry before using it. We purchased a moisture meter which has virtually eliminated shrinkage problems.

Pattern Use

Two projects in this book, the Brown Pelican and the Puppy in the Basket, include patterns and step-by-step instructions. The remaining ten projects include patterns and notes for laying out, sawing and shaping. We feel that after making the two projects featured in the first chapters, you will have a basic understanding of the techniques involved in making Intarsia. Our goal is to help you learn how to create, shape and finish your projects without detailed instructions. After practice, you will be able to look at a piece and visualize what the finished project will look like. If you do not like the way the first one came out, make another one and do things differently. I hate to give out specific thicknesses because it takes away from you learning on your own. Next thing you know, you are sanding a little, then measuring, over and over again. It can really take the fun out of a project. On many projects, if I am not very familiar with the subject matter, I will get some books from the library and have them out with me while I am shaping the piece.

The patterns are, however, marked with some very important information. On them you'll find a percentage for copying the pattern on a photocopier. Most often, the percentage is at 100% of the original. But at times, you may find a percentage for reducing or enlarging the pattern. The patterns are also marked with wood color. A legend off to the side tells you what wood color each letter stands for. You'll also find basic notes addressing special color and grain concerns and techniques. A small black-and-white drawing will help to give you some perspective on the finished piece.

In conjunction with the patterns, be sure to refer often to the color photograph of the piece on which you are working. Photos are most helpful and will give you guidelines for colors of wood, sanding heights and grain direction. As you become more familiar with Intarsia, you may even look at one of the photographs of our pieces and decide to alter the pattern or change the use of wood colors.

I think one of the most important tools (other than saws and sanders) is the use of a pencil to mark the patterns and the sides of the parts indicating their thickness next to the other parts. It is also helpful to have the complete project near where you are sanding. I have a small table on wheels I roll over to my sander, then if I have a doubt as far as where the part goes I can easily look over and see. The same old rule applies here—measure twice and cut once—in our case it is measure twice and sand once. However, in our case, if too much is sanded off, you can raise it from behind with a shim as long as it is not a part that has an outside edge.

Brown Pelican

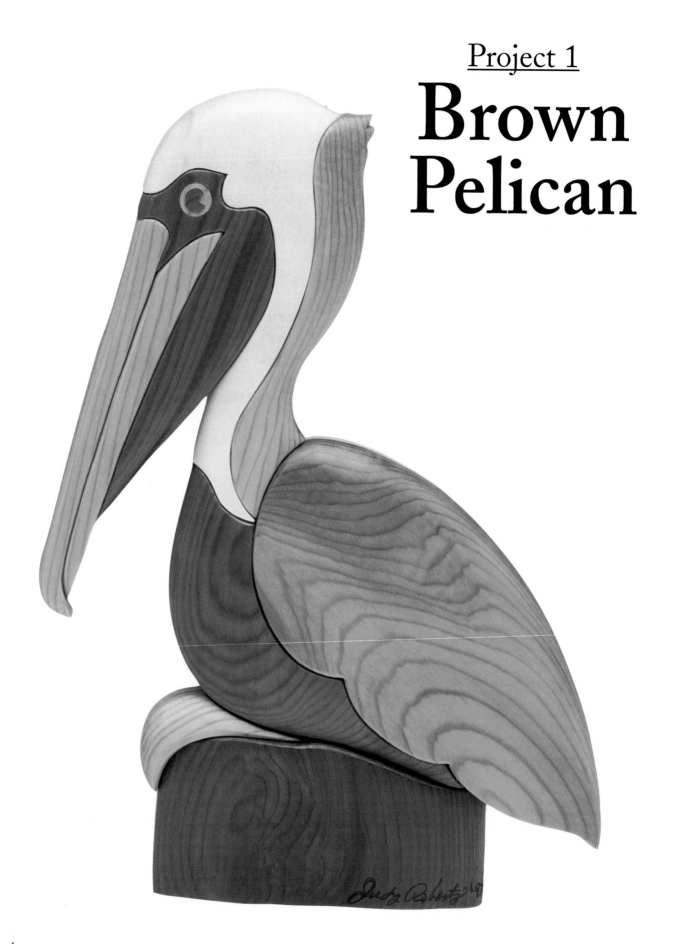

"BROWN PELICAN"

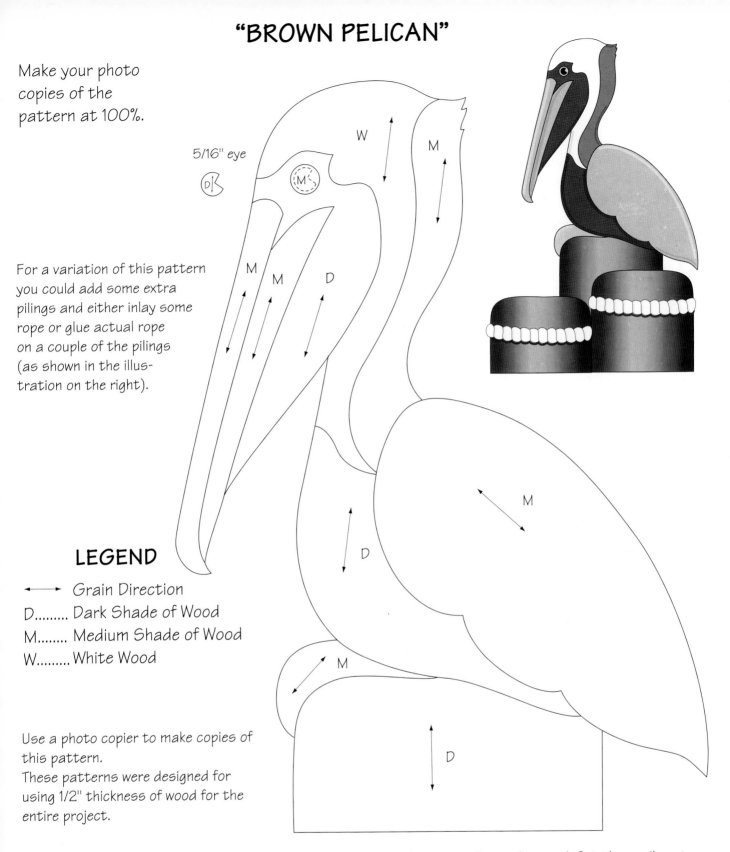

Make your photo copies of the pattern at 100%.

5/16" eye

For a variation of this pattern you could add some extra pilings and either inlay some rope or glue actual rope on a couple of the pilings (as shown in the illustration on the right).

LEGEND

⟷ Grain Direction
D......... Dark Shade of Wood
M........ Medium Shade of Wood
W........ White Wood

Use a photo copier to make copies of this pattern.
These patterns were designed for using 1/2" thickness of wood for the entire project.

You can use a dowel for the eye or cut the circular part out of some medium color wood. Cut the pupil part from a dark piece of wood. After the the area has been sanded you can glue the pupil on top of the circular medium part. After the glue dries sand it down to a little less than 1/16". Please read the following pages for detailed instructions.

I like to find a really unusal piece of wood for the wing. This pattern would look great enlarged. Also you could make the pelican facing left or right.

Project 1: Brown Pelican

MATERIALS

At least 5 copies of the pattern
Spray adhesive (repositional is best)
3 shades of wood (including a white wood)
Double-sided tape (carpet tape)
Plywood for backing ($1/8$" to $1/4$")
Clear finishing material
Woodworkers glue

STEP ONE
Laying Out The Pattern

It is always a good idea to study the pattern before jumping in. If this is your first Intarsia project, take a look at the pattern and note there are grain directions, color recommendations and areas that are raised. A legend printed on the pattern shows what each letter means. I look at my pattern and try to get a strategy as far as which colors to layout first. Is there any special wood I have tucked away that would be perfect for this project? For the pelican, the wing could use some exotic-looking grain configuration.

For these small projects I chose to use wood that is $1/2$" thick. Smaller-sized projects look very dimensional using only $1/2$"-thick material. On larger projects, I will use up to 2"-thick material to create the depth needed to keep the project from looking flat.

Because you'll be cutting out each section of the pattern separately and leaving a little extra paper around the edges, you'll need at least five copies of the pelican pattern. Save one pattern to use as your master pattern. Number each of the parts on the pattern, **(Photo 1.1)** then put the same number on each pattern section. Cut the pattern into sections, leaving some space around each section. **(Photo 1.2)** Parts like the "M" on the beak can remain together and be cut apart later on the saw. As a general rule of thumb, if the wood grain and the color are the same, those sections can be laid out as one piece and then segmented on the saw. **(Photo 1.3)** The dark portion of the eye is glued on top of the circular medium color part, so you will need to lay out both parts of the pattern. (You could use a $5/16$" dowel for the eye, but we will discuss this in more detail later in this chapter.) We have found it

helpful to mark on the pattern pieces which areas are outside edges, because these areas do not have to fit against any other part and you can relax a little when cutting them. We use arrows to mark the extent of the outside edge. **(Photo 1.4)**

After all the pattern parts have been cut out, you are ready to spray-adhesive the back of the patterns and apply them to the wood. I separate the pattern pieces by the color of the wood needed, then apply all the medium parts to one board, all the dark parts to a dark board, and so on for each color of wood. When applying the pattern to the wood note the grain direction. You can often "eye ball" some interesting grain patterns before you put the pattern down. I'll lay the pattern pieces on the board first to get a general placement, loosely mark each area, then spray the pattern parts with adhesive and apply them to the wood. **(Photo 1.5)**

STEP TWO
Using a Scroll Saw

The methods of sawing covered in this book are for the scroll saw, although this in no way implies that you must use a scroll saw. If you decide to use a band saw, a $1/16$" blade should allow you to make all the necessary cuts.

We assume that readers have good, basic scroll saw skills. If you are just beginning to scroll saw, I would suggest that you obtain one or more of the scroll saw books listed in the reference section at the back of this book to familiarize yourself with the different techniques. In addition to books, you need to practice, practice, practice. There is no substitute for a large pile of wood, plenty of sharp blades and hours upon hours of practical scroll sawing.

The blade you choose to be your favorite is a personal thing. I have talked to countless scroll sawers and it seems that we all have a favorite blade that we like to use most. Although just one single blade type will not be adequate for all types of sawing, it seems that we all return to our favorite. My personal choice is a #2 regular-tooth blade. Some people seem to think that this blade is a little small for most applications, but it

1.1 Number each of the parts on the pattern. This marked-up pattern will become your master pattern. You will want to refer to it throughout the project.

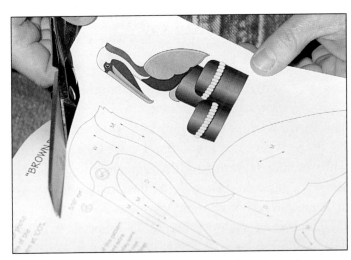

1.2 Cut the pattern into parts. Do not cut directly on the pattern lines. Instead, leave some extra space around each part. You'll need several copies in order to cut each part in this manner.

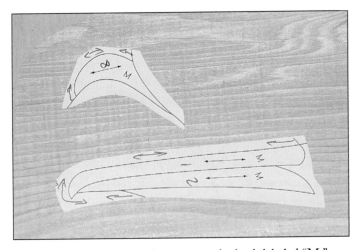

1.3 Certain parts, such as the parts on the beak labeled "M," can be laid out in one section, then cut up into individual pieces. Both the grain direction and the color need to be identical to use this technique.

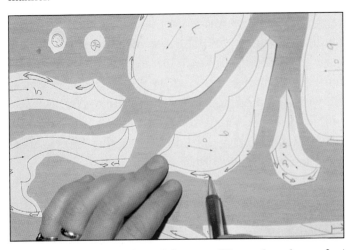

1.4 Mark the outside edges of the parts. These edges do not fit against any other part and will not need to be cut quite as precisely as the inside edges.

1.5 Lay the pattern pieces on the wood to get a general feel of how you want to cut the parts. Pay close attention to any interesting grain patterns. Loosely mark each area, then use spray adhesive to apply the pattern pieces to the wood.

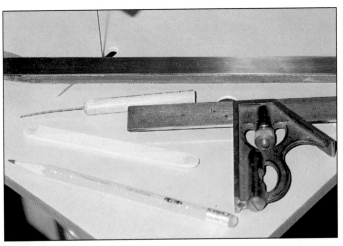

1.6 Some make-shift tools can come in handy while you are sawing the parts. A modified popsicle stick holds down the edges of the pattern, and a dowel fitted with a scroll saw blade pushes out inside drop-out pieces of wood. A 6" square helps to check parts for squareness.

Project 1: Brown Pelican

has worked well for me and is my blade of choice. I used a #2 for these Intarsia miniatures exclusively, except in areas that call for a vein to be cut, in which case I used a larger (wider) blade.

Shown here are tools that I have close at hand while sawing. **(Photo 1.6)** I have tapered the rounded ends of a popsicle stick to hold down the paper pattern as I saw. Even though the pattern has been applied to the wood with a spray adhesive, at times the pattern will have a tendency to flap a little. I use the stick to hold down the flapping pattern instead of using my finger. The second tool is a piece of a scroll saw blade that I have fitted into the end of a dowel and glued. I use this as a push rod when doing fret work. It helps me to remove the inside dropout piece. I also have a sanding block on my table, or more recently, I have been using the flat Intarsia Detail Sander. I use this to remove the burr on the bottom side of the work piece, allowing the piece to sit flat on the table. And last but not least, I have a 6" square to check my parts for squareness. The square and the sander are the two most important tools I use when cutting.

When sitting down for a work session, along with lining up my tools, I will also check my machine for squareness, just in case I or someone else has tilted the table since the last time it was used. While the machine is turned off, I check the blade's squareness to the table by using a small square. I have found that this is a good place to start, however, the proof is in the cut. So, after checking the squareness with a small square, I make a cut across a piece of $3/4$" to 1" thick stock and check the cut for squareness. **(Photo 1.7)** Should the new cut across the piece of wood be out-of-square, I make another cut the same way and check it again.

When checking the squareness with this method, it is important to remove any burr on the bottom of the wood before starting the cut. This ensures that the wood is sitting flat on the table and is not rocking or sitting at an angle, even before the test cut is made. If I am satisfied that the saw is cutting square, I then proceed. If the blade is out-of-square with the table, now is the time to make an adjustment to the table to bring it back into square with the blade. After any adjust-

ment to the table, I always take another cut and check it for squareness, repeating the steps above until I am satisfied with the squareness.

Although I try to make my cuts square, I have found that it is almost impossible to maintain squareness at all times because of the burr that is created on the bottom side of the wood during cutting. There is, however, a "happy medium" that I have found for my cutting. You will also find your happy medium for out-of-squareness. Out-of-squareness can also be caused by operator error (in fact that is my biggest problem). Too much cutting pressure or not feeding the wood directly into the face of the blade are other reasons for out-of-square cuts.

It really does not matter which part you start cutting first, however, I usually start with the easiest one first. This allows me to get into the swing of things. Although I am only cutting one $1/2$" thickness it is still important to check for squareness. **(Photo 1.8)** Many of these projects can be stack cut, which means cutting two pieces at the same time. If you do stack cut, it is important to stay as square as possible to insure a good fit. You can stack cut two different colors of wood and exchange the parts to make two differently colored projects, or you can stack cut two pieces of the same color, which will provide parts for two identical projects.

Before starting to cut a part, turn it over and remove any burr that may be present. **(Photo 1.9)** When sawing, I try to keep the center of my #2 scroll saw blade on the center of the line, completely removing any trace of the line, providing the line is a thin one. **(Photo 1.10)** If the line is thicker than the blade, still try to stay in the center of the line, leaving an equal amount of line on each side of the cut.

Note the red arrows around the outside of the wing. **(Photo 1.11)** The arrows indicate that this edge does not fit against another part. It is always a good idea to be aware of which edge is an outside edge and which edge butts up against another piece.

Here the burr is being removed from the backside of the wing after the first cut has been made. **(Photo 1.12)** This allows the part to sit flat on the table before

1.7 Before beginning to cut out the parts, first check the saw for squareness. Make a cut across a piece of 3/4"–1" thick stock. If it is not square, adjust the saw and make another cut. Continue checking the saw for squareness until the saw makes a nice 90° cut.

1.8 Start cutting whichever part appears to be the easiest for you to cut. As you cut, continue to check your parts for squareness. Parts that are out-of-square will not fit correctly against the other parts in the Intarsia design.

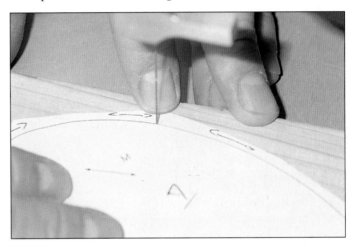

1.9 Before starting to cut a part, turn the part over and remove any burr that may be present. The Detail Sander works great for removing burrs. Sandpaper stapled to a piece of wood works well also.

1.10 While sawing, keep the center of the scroll saw blade in the center of the line. This will remove any trace of a thin line. If your line is thicker, still try to stay in the center of the line, leaving an equal amount of line on each side of the cut.

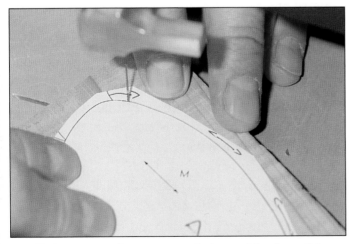

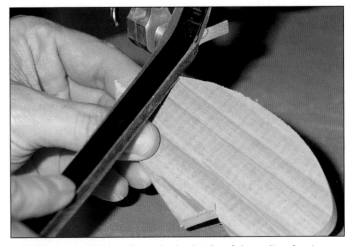

1.11 Red arrows on the pattern mark the outside edges of the parts. These arrows indicate edges that do not fit against any other part. While you still want to cut all your parts carefully, you do not have to cut these edges quite so precisely.

1.12 Remove the burr from the backside of the pelican's wing after making the first cut. This will ensure that the part will lay flat on the saw when you make the second cut. Always remember to remove any burr before progressing to the next cut. otherwise you run the risk of your parts being out-of-square.

Intarsia Artistry

Project 1: Brown Pelican

the second cut is made. Also shown is the Intarsia Detail Sander, mentioned earlier.

For the bottom section of the wing where one rounded section ends and another one begins, a quick turn will allow for an almost sharp corner. **(Photo 1.13)**

To create the eye, you have two choices: 1) Drill a hole and use a dowel for the eye, or 2) thread a scroll saw blade into a drilled hole and saw out the eye. Here I chose to saw the eye rather than use a large drill. **(Photo 1.14)** Note that I am sawing the eye first before I saw the outside section of the head. If you are using a band saw, you will have to drill the eye to size and use a dowel.

After all the parts have been cut out, the burr on the bottom of each piece is then sanded off, allowing the parts to sit flat. **(Photo 1.15)** On the back of each piece, print the numbers that correspond to the numbers assigned earlier to each part. Numbering the parts is a good habit to develop, especially when working on projects that have many parts.

STEP THREE
Shaping the Pelican

It is helpful to have some type of sander for this step. When I started out, all we used was a belt sander and a disc sander. The only problem with these sanders is the metal backing, which makes for a very hard surface. This makes it much more difficult to get soft, rounded contours. However, it is still possible to use these sanders. Any type of sander is better than none at all. Now, I use an inflatable drum sander (pneumatic) that has two drums. There are a number of differently sized drums available. For these smaller projects it is helpful to have a smaller drum, 2" to 3" in diameter. I like to have one drum with 100-grit paper and the other with a well worn 120-grit paper. I use the 100-grit to rough in the parts and the 120-grit to clean them up. If you are using hard woods, such as walnut, maple or oak, you may want to start with 80-grit.

There is a reasonably priced sander called a Flex Drum sander. It has a foam pad that works like the pneumatic sanders. The little drum sanders you see in many of the woodworking catalogs will also work. Many of those drums have a hard rubber drum with the sanding sleeve wrapped around it. The pneumatic and the Flex Sander have some give to them.

After all the parts are cut out, I assemble the project and check it to make sure it fits. **(Photo 1.16)** It may be a good idea to leave the pattern on the wood, in case a part needs to be trimmed. If everything fits correctly, remove the paper pattern from the face of the wood. You are now ready to shape each part with the sander.

The object I keep in mind while shaping is that I will be lowering, or sanding down, individual parts to make the adjoining parts stand out. I take a moment before I begin sanding to study the design and make a mental plan of action. Many times there are sections that can be sanded together, as if they were one piece of wood. On the pelican, you can sand the head and the beak sections together. Trace around these parts onto a piece of scrap plywood. **(Photo 1.17)** This piece of plywood will act as a sanding shim, holding the pieces together as you sand. I like to cut my shims ahead of time so that when I start sanding I will not have to stop the flow of work. **(Photo 1.18)**

For the pelican, I sanded the foot part first, rounding the upper part toward the body. **(Photo 1.19)** I then use a pencil to mark where the foot joins the body. **(Photo 1.20)** The use of a pencil throughout the entire sanding process is extremely helpful. Then I rounded the piling toward the outside edges **(Photo 1.21)** and marked with pencil where the piling joins the body. Next I sanded the body, being careful not sand below the mark I made for the foot. If you like, you can sand the body below the level of the piling just a small amount. I sanded mine a little below the piling. Try not to round the area where the body joins the neck section. You will want to lower the body section down to give the wing some depth. I sanded the pelican's body down to a little over $3/8$" thick, then rounded it toward the outside. **(Photo 1.22)** Next I marked where the body joins the wing and the neck area.

Now let's prepare the neck, head and beak area using the sanding shim made earlier. To attach the

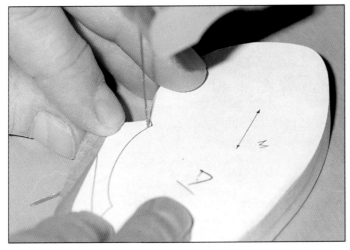

1.13 Make a quick turn at the bottom section of the wing to make an almost-sharp corner. Here one rounded section ends and another one begins.

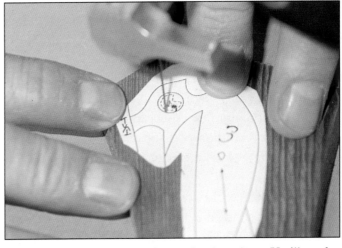

1.14 Use a scroll saw to cut the eye for the pelican. You'll need to drill a small hole through which the scroll saw blade will be threaded. Bandsaw users may opt to drill the eye and insert a dowel.

1.15 Check the bottom of the cut-out parts one more time. Sand away any burr that remains so that all the parts will sit flat. Refer to your master pattern to print the pattern numbers on the back of each part.

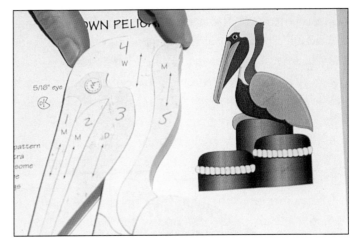

1.16 Leave the pattern pieces on the wood, and assemble the project to make sure all the parts fit correctly. Trim any pieces that need to be adjusted, then remove the paper pattern from the wood.

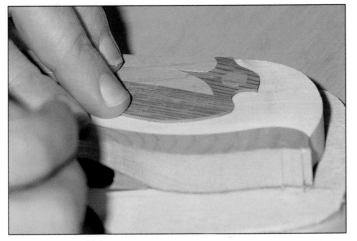

1.17 Decide which parts should be sanded together and make a sanding shim. For the pelican, the head and beak parts can be sanded together. Place these parts on a piece of scrap plywood and trace around them.

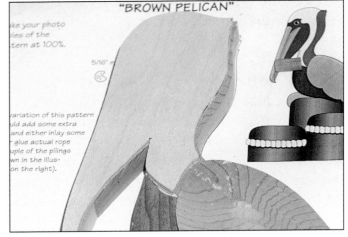

1.18 Cut out the plywood to make the sanding shim. When it is time to sand the head and the beak, we will glue the parts to the sanding shim. (I find it a good idea to cut the sanding shims ahead of time, so I don't have to interrupt my work flow later.)

Project 1: Brown Pelican

wood to the shim, I use an inexpensive double-sided carpet tape cut into thin strips. **(Photo 1.23)** I apply the least amount possible to hold the parts together. **(Photo 1.24)** Sometimes you can easily break parts if the bond between the wood and the tape is too strong. Put the sanding shim in place, and now the pieces are ready to sand.

The neck/head/beak section will be done in two steps. First round the beak and the head sections together. **(Photo 1.25)** Then take off the beak section **(Photo 1.26)** and taper the neck down toward the body, using the pencil line as a guide. **(Photo 1.27)** Put the beak section back in place and mark where the neck joins the beak. **(Photo 1.28)** Round the beak section down toward the neck, **(Photo 1.29)** again using the pencil line as a guide. Remove all the parts from the sanding shim and mark where the neck joins the wing. When sanding the wing be careful not to sand below the pencil lines for the neck and body sections. **(Photo 1.30)** I tapered the wing toward the back, then rounded the outside edge. **(Photo 1.31)** After you are satisfied with the shaping, finish sand all the parts with 220-grit sandpaper.

Now let's glue the pupil part on the eye. You can turn the gleam of the eye in any direction you want. Glue the pupil on the eye, **(Photo 1.32)** and once the glue is dry, you can sand it down to a little less than $1/16$". **(Photo 1.33)** Lightly sand the edge of each part to remove the sharp edge. I sanded the face of each part with 220-grit paper. Then I used an air compressor to blow the dust off each part.

STEP FOUR
Applying the Finish

After all the parts have peen sanded, checked for scratches, de-burred and dusted off, it is time to put a clear finish on the parts. I put the finish on before I glue the pieces down. It is easier to get a nice finish this way. Also when you are gluing the project down to the backing, glue that has been dropped on a piece is easier to wipe off of a finished surface.

I use Bartley Wiping Gel to finish the parts. It is a polyurethane in a gel base. I apply two coats of clear satin, waiting at least 4 hours before applying the next coat. For the final coat, we use a matte Bartley Wiping Gel made especially for me and Judy.

We prefer a matte or a more satin finish as opposed to a very shiny finish, but this is strictly a personal choice. It is up to you what type of finish you prefer. There are many types of finish you can use, but whatever you chose be sure to follow the directions.

If you decide to use the Bartley Gel, keep the following tips in mind. The first coat is the most time consuming. The longer the gel is exposed to air, the quicker it will form a "skin" on the top layer. I find it a good idea to turn the lid of the can upside down and work off of the lid. Just take the lid off and put a small amount of Bartley on the underside of the lid, then put the lid over the top of the can. **(Photo 1.34)** I like to apply the finish to the face of the part and on all of the sides, but not the bottom, which is where the glue will be applied. **(Photo 1.35)**

This step moves very quickly if there are two people working together. One puts the finish on and the other wipes it off. If you are working by yourself just put the finish on about three to four parts then go back and start to wipe off the parts before applying gel to more parts.

I use sponge brushes to apply the finish and paper towels to wipe it off. **(Photo 1.36)** Leave the finish on for about a minute or so, then wipe it dry. If the gel gets sticky, you may have let it set too long before wiping it off. In this case, apply a fresh coat to soften up the sticky gel and then wipe the surface clean. Be sure to keep using a fresh part of the paper towel and change the towel frequently. The more worn the towel gets, the greater the chance of it leaving lint on the surface of the part.

After all the parts have been coated, wait at least four hours before applying the second coat. Depending on the humidity, it may take longer for the first coat of gel to dry. Feel the sides of the parts and the face. If they are not tacky, then go ahead and apply the second coat. After the second coat is dry, check the face of each part. Sometimes the white wood isn't as smooth as it could be. We go over any parts that are a

1.19 Now you are ready to begin sanding. First, sand the foot part, rounding the upper part toward the body.

1.20 On the body, use a pencil to mark the height at which the foot meets the body. This line will act as a guide later when you begin sanding the body.

1.21 Next, round the piling toward the outside edges. Again, mark on the body the height at which the piling meets the body.

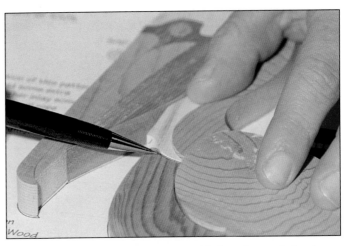

1.22 Now sand the body. Do not sand below the mark for the foot. If you choose, you may want to sand below the mark for the piling. Sand the entire body down to $3/8"$. Mark where the body joins the wing and the neck.

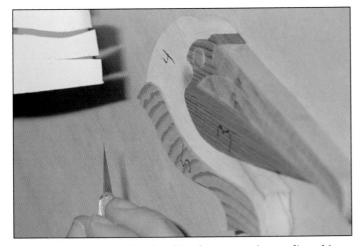

1.23 Attach the neck, head and beak parts to the sanding shim using double-sided carpet tape cut into thin strips.

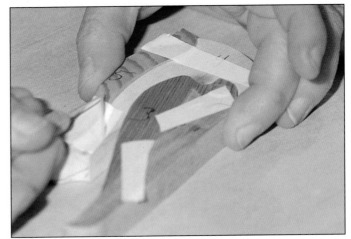

1.24 Use the least amount possible to hold the pieces in place. You want to be able to remove the parts from the shim easily once the sanding is complete.

Project 1: Brown Pelican

little rough with a "00" steel wool before the final coat. Be sure to remove any steel fibers that may have been left behind before applying the final coat.

STEP FIVE
Cutting the Backing

When the finish is dry, it's time to layout the backing. I trace around the actual project to get an outline for the backing rather than using the pattern. Sometimes during the sanding process, pieces become altered or perhaps fit better with the head turned a little. Tracing around the actual project ensures that the backing will match the project exactly.

Note: If you are planning to mount the pelican (or any Intarsia project) to something like a jewelry box, letter holder or some other type of project, it is not necessary to make a backing. Just glue the pieces directly to the face of the project.

I do my layout on a piece of paper. (Photo 1.37) It helps to spray a very light coat of spray adhesive on the paper and then place the parts on top; the adhesive keeps the parts from sliding around while you trace the pelican. Then remove the parts and apply the pattern to a 1/8" plywood board with spray adhesive. I've found that Baltic or Finnish birch works great.

When cutting the backing stay to the inside of the pencil line. You will want the backing slightly smaller than the actual pelican.

After de-burring the backing, you can put a dark stain around the edges. This will help to hide the edges and draw less attention to the backing. I did not stain the edges on these projects. Also, if there are any gaps, it helps to stain the space between the parts. Then we seal the back side with a clear acrylic spray.

STEP SIX
Gluing the Pelican Down

The pelican is now ready to glue down to the backing. Place the parts on the backing and check all the edges to make sure no backing is exposed. (Photo 1.38) If the backing is showing, you will need to mark those areas and trim them on your saw.

Pick a few key parts to lock the project in place.

The piling would be a good locking part. (Photo 1.39) I put dots of wood glue, leaving space for a few dots of hot glue. Using two different types of glue is important. The hot glue sets quickly and works like a clamp. This will help anchor the project and keep the pieces from shifting as you continue.

Use a few dots of hot glue to work as a clamp. (Photo 1.40) If you are using hot glue, you have to move fast and accurately before the glue sets up. Five to ten seconds is all the time you'll have before the glue sets up. Put the piling in place and apply pressure to the part until the hot glue sets up. (Photo 1.41) After the piling is set, continue gluing the rest of the pelican down. I would use the same combination (mostly wood glue with a few dots of hot glue) on all the parts, except the foot. Use just use a little wood glue on the foot. After the glue sets up use a hanger of your choice.

There are several different types of hangers to use. We use a mirror hanger and a small screw on many of our projects. You could use small saw tooth hangers and use a stapler or the small nails to put the hanger on the project.

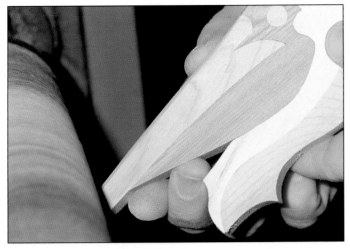

1.25 Sand the neck, head and beak parts in two steps. First, round the beak and the head sections together.

1.26 Next, remove the beak part from the shim. Do this carefully. Parts can be easily broken if too much force is applied.

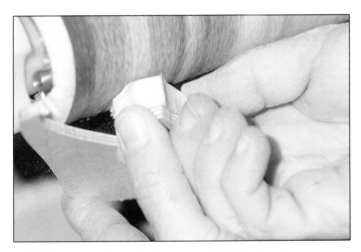

1.27 Now, taper the neck down toward the body using your pencil line as a guide.

1.28 Put the beak part back in place and mark where the neck joins the beak.

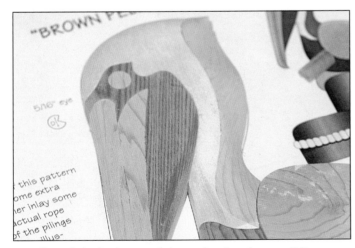

1.29 Round the beak toward the neck using the pencil line as a guide.

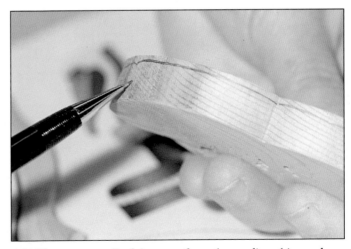

1.30 Now remove all of the parts from the sanding shim and mark where the neck joins the wing. Be careful not to sand below the pencil lines for the neck and body sections.

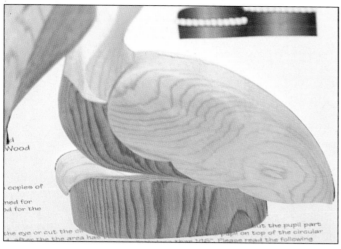

1.31 Taper the wing toward the back, then round the outside edge. Once you are satisfied with the shape of the parts, finish sand them with 220-grit sandpaper and blow off the dust with compressed air.

1.32 Glue the pupil part on the eye, placing the "gleam" in any direction you like.

1.33 When the glue is dry, sand the gleam down to a little less than 1/16". Lightly sand the edge of each part to remove the sharp edge.

1.34 Finish the parts with a clear finish before you assemble the pelican. For this demonstration, we used Bartley Wiping Gel. Put a small amount in the inside of the lid and then place the lid on top of the can.

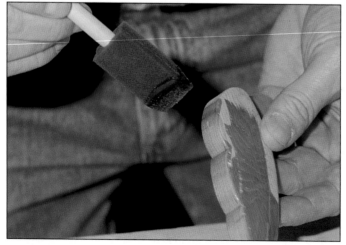

1.35 Using a sponge brush, apply clear satin Bartley Wiping Gel to the top and sides of all the parts. Do not apply the gel to the bottom of the parts.

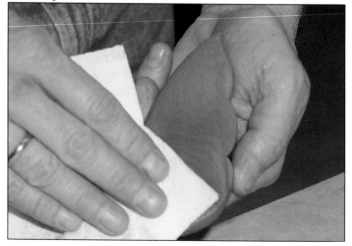

1.36 After a minute or so, wipe off the gel with a clean paper towel. Apply another coat of clear satin gel, wipe it off, wait at least four hours, then apply a coat of matte wiping gel to give the pieces a nice matte finish.

Intarsia Artistry

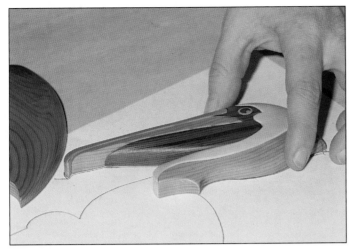

1.37 To create the backing, first apply spray adhesive to a piece of paper and layout the parts on this paper. Trace around the pelican. Remove the parts, then apply the paper to a piece of 1/8" plywood and cut it to shape.

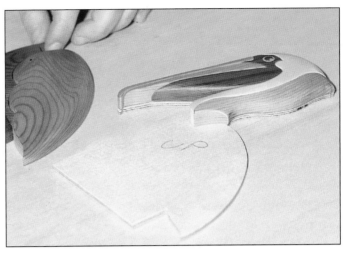

1.38 Place the parts on the backing and check all the edges to make sure that no backing is exposed. Trim any exposed areas on the saw.

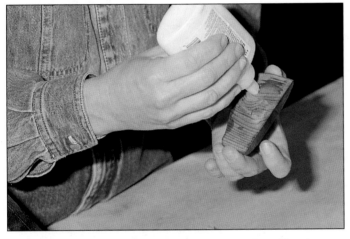

1.39 Pick a few pieces to "lock" the project in place. For the pelican, the piling is a good locking piece.

1.40 Apply a thin bead of wood glue and a few drops of hot glue to the back of the part. The hot glue sets up quickly, within five to ten seconds, and will act as a clamp.

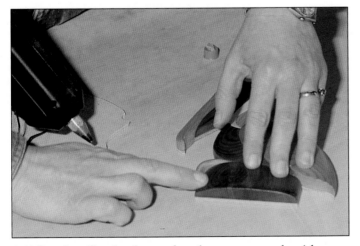

1.41 Put the piling in place and apply pressure evenly with your hands until the hot glue sets up. Continue gluing the other parts to the backing in the same manner.

Puppy in a Basket

"Puppy in a Basket"

There a some ways to simplify this pattern. Please see page 34 for more details.

This puppy can be adapted to look like many different types of dogs. The Dalmatian would be one of the more challenging to make.

Eye detail enlarged to show color.

You can use the patterns above for making the shims to raise portions of this pattern. You can raise areas in sections rather than one piece at a time.

LEGEND

→ ..... Grain Direction
D........ Dark Shade of Wood
MD...... Medium Dark Shade of Wood
M........ Medium Shade of Wood
W........ White Wood
R........ Raise these areas 1/8"

Make your photo copies of the pattern at 100%.

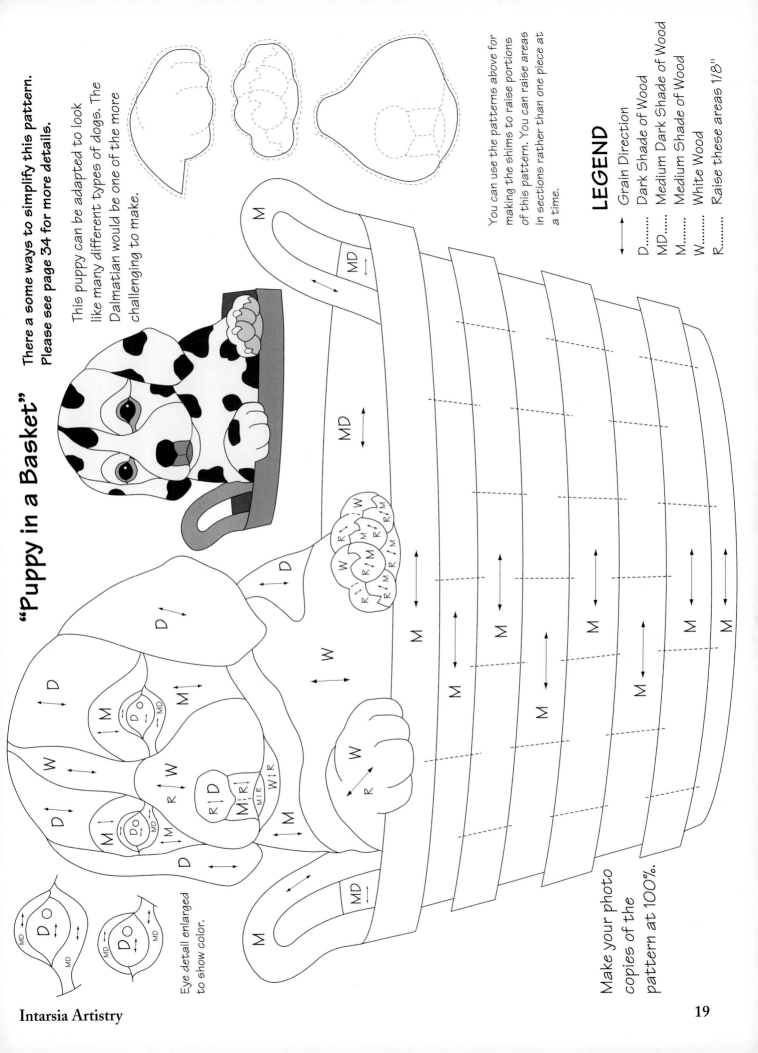

Project 2: Puppy in a Basket

MATERIALS
At least 6 copies of the pattern
Spray adhesive (repositional is best)
4 shades of wood (including a white wood)
Double-sided tape (carpet tape)
Plywood for backing (¹/₈" to ¹/₄")
Clear finishing material
Woodworkers glue
Wood burner (optional)

STEP ONE
Laying Out the Pattern
Glance over the pattern and look at the photo of the finished piece to get an idea of the colors of wood you want to use. I recommend four different shades: dark (D), medium-dark (MD), medium (M) and white. If you want to use different medium-colored (M) woods for the basket and the puppy, you'll need to choose a fifth shade. Be creative with your choice of woods. I used ¹/₂" thick material for this project.

2.1 Cut the pattern for the puppy in the basket into sections, leaving some space around each part. You'll need at least six copies of the pattern to accomplish this task.

You can stack cut some sections of this pattern, however, I chose to cut the parts singularly.

Make at least six copies of the pattern. Save one pattern to use as your master pattern and number each of the parts on this pattern. Cut one section for each different part of the pattern, leaving some space around each part. **(Photo 2.1)** Transfer the same numbers from the master pattern to each pattern section. **(Photo 2.2)** Parts like the "M" on the basket can remain together then cut on the saw. **(Photo 2.3)**

After all the pattern parts have been cut out you are ready to glue the patterns to the wood. I separate the pattern pieces by color, then apply all the medium parts to one board, all the dark parts to a dark board, and so on for each color of wood. When applying the pattern to the wood, note the grain direction as indicated by the arrows on the patterns. I'll put the parts on the board first to get a general placement, loosely mark each area, then apply a spray adhesive to the pattern parts and apply them to the wood.

For the basket, if you have a piece of wood that goes from a medium-light shade to a medium shade, you can put the lighter side toward the top of the basket, which will add more dimension. **(Photo 2.4)** I used aspen for the white wood. You any kind of white wood, including white pine or holly. The puppy in this project could take on many different

2.2 Keep one pattern intact to use as a master pattern. Number all the parts on this pattern, then transfer those numbers to the cut-out pattern pieces.

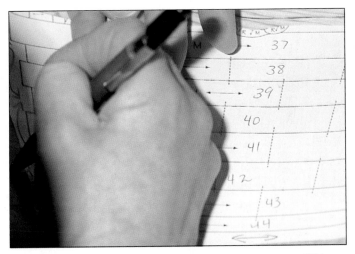

2.3 Number the parts on the back of the master pattern. This organizational step will help you keep the parts in order once they have been cut out and save you time later.

2.4 A wood that changes from a medium light shade to a medium shade could be used for the basket. Use the lighter area for the top edge of the basket.

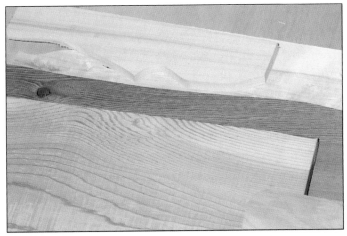

2.5 Gather any available wood together so you can plan which shades to use for the puppy in the basket. You'll need at least four; five if you want the puppy and the basket to be different shades.

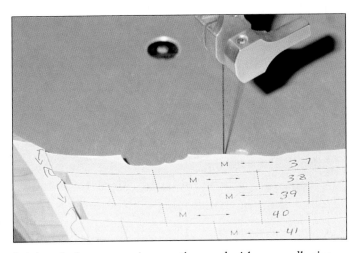

2.6 Attach the pattern pieces to the wood with spray adhesive. Saw the outside of the basket first, noting the red arrows that indicate the outside edge of the part.

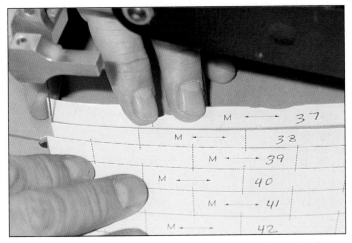

2.7 When the basket is sawed out, come back and cut the slats.

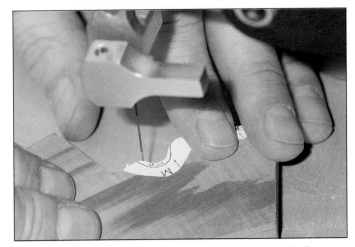

2.8 Take care when sawing the upper and lower eyelids. Extra wood should be left on small pieces such as these to give you a piece of wood to hold.

Project 2: Puppy in a Basket

colors, perhaps a dark puppy with white spots. Try stack cutting this project and make two at a time if you wish.

STEP TWO
Sawing the Puppy

Sawing the puppy in the basket is another pretty straight-forward project to cut out. **(Photo 2.5)**

Here I chose to saw the outside portion of the basket **(Photo 2.6)** then come back and cut the slats. **(Photo 2.7)** Again note the red arrows indicating the outside edges of the project that do not fit next to another part.

Care should be taken when sawing the upper and lower eyelids. **(Photo 2.8)** When sawing small parts, always allow yourself a nice-sized piece of wood to hang on to. Plan ahead to allow yourself enough wood to grip, instead of winding up with a piece too small to hold. For the eyelids I elected to make the inside cut first. Note that I have a piece of thin plywood placed under the part for the second cut. **(Photo 2.9)** Once the part is cut, this thin piece of plywood will prevent the small piece from falling through the slot in the table and becoming lost or damaged.

After cutting the puppy's paw (his right one), I came back and did the veining (the cuts between the toes) with a larger #9 blade, which better defines the

toes. **(Photo 2.10)**

After all the parts have been cut out, remove the burr from the back of the parts and put a number on each piece. **(Photo 2.11)**

STEP THREE
Shaping the Puppy

If you did not make the pelican, please read the section on "Shaping the Pelican" in the previous chapter for information about the different types of sanders that work best for Intarsia.

After all the parts are cut out, assemble the project and check to make sure the pieces fit. **(Photo 2.12)** It may be a good idea to leave the pattern on the wood, in case a part needs to be trimmed. If everything fits correctly, remove the paper pattern from the face of the wood.

The object I keep in mind while shaping is that I will be lowering (or sanding down) parts to make the adjoining parts stand out. I take a moment at this time to study the design and make a little mental plan of action. Many times there are sections that can be sanded together, as if they were one piece of wood. On the puppy you can sand parts of the head, the body section and the basket together. **(Photo 2:13)**

Trace around the parts you'll be sanding together onto a piece of scrap plywood (or use the pattern

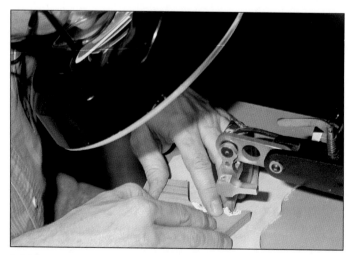

2.9 Place a piece of thin plywood under the part for the second eyelid cut. The plywood will keep the small piece from falling through the slot in the table once it is cut out.

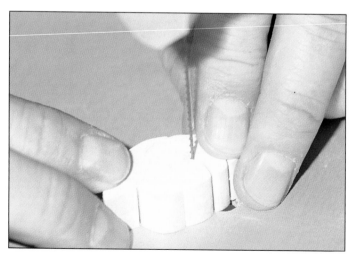

2.10 Cut the puppy's paw, then do the cuts between the toes with a larger #9 blade. This blade will better define the toes.

2.11 Remove the burr from the back of the parts after each cut to ensure that the pieces lie flat. Transfer the numbers from the master pattern to each part again, if needed.

2.12 When all the parts are cut, assemble the project and check the parts to make sure each fits correctly. Leave the pattern pieces on the wood in case any of the parts need to be trimmed.

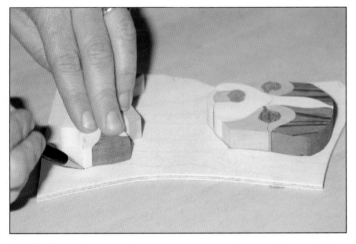

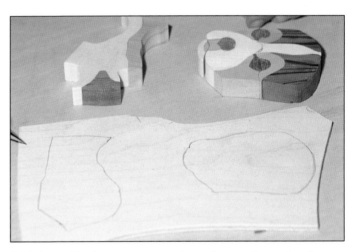

2.13 In Intarsia, sometimes there are parts that can be sanded together. On the puppy, the head, the body section and the basket can be sanded together.

2.14 Assemble these parts on a piece of scrap plywood and trace around them. The plywood will act as a sanding shim, holding the pieces in place while you sand.

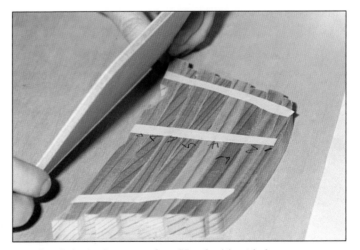

2.15 When sanding raised areas, such as the two paws and the nose, be sure to include the $1/8$" shim when you sand. After cutting the shims for these areas, put them in place now.

2.16 Sand the basket parts first. Use double-sided carpet tape to hold the basket parts to the sanding shim.

2.17 Sand these pieces together to get the basic shape. First, round the basket toward the outside edges, but not all the way over.

2.18 Next, take off the upper rim of the basket. Sand down the rest of the basket parts to make them lower than the rim.

2.19 Now put the rim back to see if you have sanded away enough wood to make the rim thicker than the basket.

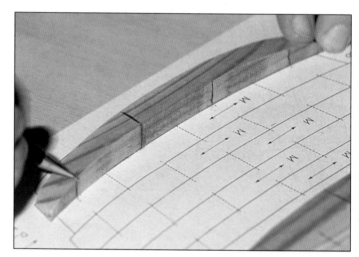

2.20 To sand the dips in the basket, first mark where the dips are located on the face and sides of the basket.

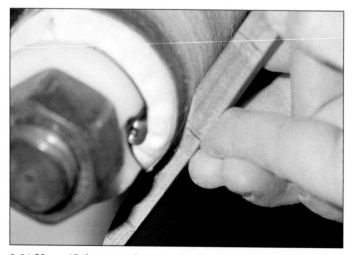

2.21 Use a 2" drum sander to make the dips. Alternately, you can carve the dips with a file or use the edge of a disc sander.

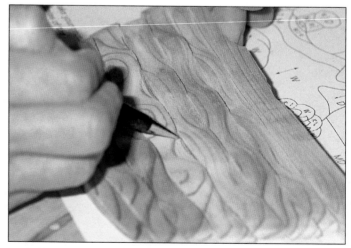

2.22 Alternate the dips with the adjoining parts to give the basket a woven appearance.

2.23 After sanding the dips, sand the back side of the basket down to about $^3/_{16}$" deep.

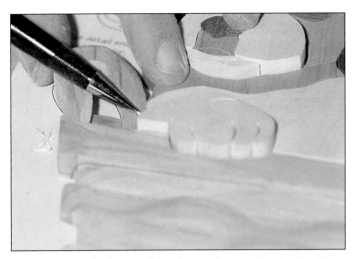

2.24 Mark the thickness of the rim on the part for the handles. Sand below this mark, but not below the mark for the back side of the basket. Round the handles toward the outside and inside edges.

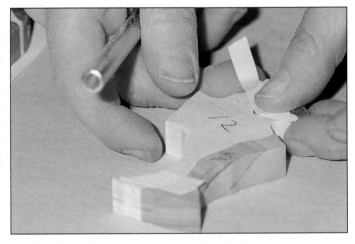

2.25 Sand the three body parts together. Apply only enough double-sided carpet tape to hold the parts together. Too much tape will create too strong a bond between parts and cause them to break when separated.

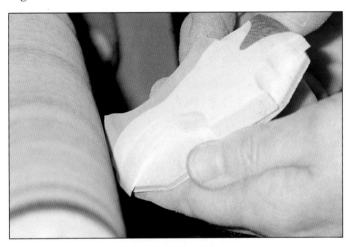

2.26 Attach the body parts to a sanding shim, again using double-sided tape only sparingly. First taper the body toward the head section. Then round the body toward the sides.

2.27 After you've finished sanding, remove the sanding shim and mark where the body parts touch the feet, head and ear sections.

2.28 Carve between the toe lines, stair stepping the toes as they go toward the body. A knife or a Wonder Wheel works well for this operation.

Project 2: Puppy in a Basket

if you have some extra pattern pieces) to make a sanding shim. **(Photo 2.14)** The shim will hold the pieces together as you sand. When it is time to sand these sections you will have your sanding shim ready to go. I like to cut my shims ahead of time so when I start sanding I will not have to stop the flow of my work.

There are several areas marked to be raised $1/8$": the two paws and the nose section. I cut those out at this time also. When sanding raised sections you will want to include the shim when you are doing the actual sanding. After cutting the shims for the raised areas, put them in place at this time. **(Photo 2.15)**

I sanded the basket parts first. **(Photo 2.16)** Using the double-sided tape, I applied the basket parts to the sanding shim. I prefer to sand them all together to get the basic shape. First just round the basket toward the outside edges. **(Photo 2.17)** Do not round the parts all the way over. You will want to leave some material, especially on the rim, so that you can sand the handles to be a little thinner than the rim. Next take off the upper rim of the basket. **(Photo 2.18)** Then sand down the rest of the basket parts to make them lower than the rim. Be sure to maintain the rounded shape. Now put the rim back to see if enough wood has been sanded away to make the rim the thicker part. **(Photo 2.19)** If there is a stair step down to the basket you can take the parts off of the sanding shim at this time.

Mark with a pencil where the basket joins the body, the feet, the handles and the back side of the basket. Now, sand the dips in the basket. Using the pattern as a guide, I marked the face and the sides where each dip is located. **(Photo 2.20)** I marked the side to make it easier to see while I was sanding. I used a 2" diameter drum sander to make the dips. **(Photo 2.21)** If you do not have a drum close to this size, you can either carve the dip with a file or use the edge of a disc sander. Be sure to pay attention to where the dips are located. You will want them to alternate with the adjoining parts to give a basket-like appearance. Go through and sand the dips in each strip. **(Photo 2.22)**

Next sand the back side of the basket (the MD sections). Sand below the mark you made for the rim, down to about $3/16$". **(Photo 2.23)** Mark with pencil where the backing touches the puppy parts and the handles. **(Photo 2.24)** Now sand the handles. You'll want to sand them down below the mark showing the thickness of the rim, but do not sand below the mark for the back side of the basket. I rounded the handles toward the outside and inside edges.

Next we are ready to sand the puppy body. I sanded the three body parts—the white, the medium, and the dark parts—together. I used an inexpensive double-sided carpet tape cut into thin strips to hold the parts to the sanding shim. I applied the least amount possible to hold the parts together. **(Photo 2.25)**

Now put the sanding shim in place, and you'll be ready to sand the body. Sand the body part down to give the head and feet more dimension. When sanding this section do not sand so much that the shim for the raised areas will be exposed (do not sand lower than $1/8$"). I tapered the body toward the head section **(Photo 2.26)**, then slightly rounded it toward the sides. **(Photo 2.27)** After sanding, remove the sanding shim and put the parts back in place. Mark where the body parts touch the feet, head and ear sections.

Next, sand the feet. Start with the solid foot first, just roughing it in as well as you can with the sander. Taper it back toward the body, leaving maximum thickness where it touches the rim of the basket. Then to get the rounded toes you will need to do some carving. I used a combination of carving with the Wonder Wheel and a X-acto Knife. Different tools work better depending on what type of wood you are using. I used all soft wood, the Wonder Wheel and the Knife work very well. Carve between the toe lines, stair stepping the toes as they go toward the body. **(Photo 2.28)** The wheel burns the wood as it removes material. These burn marks will be sanded off. **(Photo 2.29)** After you have the foot roughed in, put it back in place to see how it looks.

2.29 The Wonder Wheel burns the wood as it removes material. These burn marks will need to be sanded off later.

2.30 When the foot is roughed-out, put it back in place to see how it looks with the other pieces. You may need to do some additional sanding.

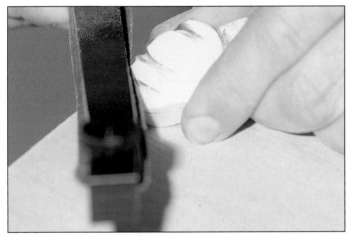

2.31 If the foot fits correctly, hand sand the part. Use a Detail Sander or hand sand with a piece of sand paper.

2.32 Sand the toes of the other foot together. Double-sided tape holds the parts to the shim.

2.33 Round the toes toward the body and a little down toward the rim. Then take the parts off the shim and sand them individually.

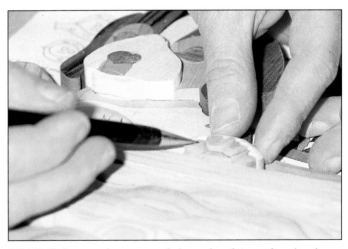

2.34 Roll the toes down toward the pad and toward each other. Mark where the pads join the upper toe parts.

Project 2: Puppy in a Basket

(Photo 2.30) If it fits correctly, go ahead and do some more hand sanding on the foot. The Detail Sander works great for this. (Photo 3.31) You can sand the rough areas by hand.

Now onto the other foot. I sanded the toes together, then took the parts and sanded them individually. I used doubled-sided tape and taped the toe parts to the shim I made to raise those parts. (Photo 2.32) Just rough in the foot, watching those pencil lines. You do not want to sand below the pencil marks. After you have the basic shape (rounded toward the body and a little down toward the rim), take the parts off the shim. (Photo 2.33)

Now start shaping the individual parts. First I lowered the lowest pad section (the part that touches the rim). Again watch those pencil guide line. Do not sand this part below the rim. If you do happen to sand a part too much, you can back track and sand the rim down a bit more, but then you may also have to re-sand some other parts. After sanding the lower pad on the foot, mark where it joins the toe pads. Roll the toes down toward the pad and toward each other. (Photo 2.34) Then mark where the pads join the upper toe parts. Round the toes and carve a groove between the toes.

Now start on the face. Sand the ear on the left side. (Photo 2.35) I sanded mine down to about $3/16$". This part also covers a shim, so do not sand it down below $1/8$". Mark where this ear joins the face. The face will be sanded in two steps. (Photo 2.36) First tape all the face parts to the sanding shim. Round the head toward the top, then blend in the raised nose area, and taper the sides of the head toward the ears. (Photo 2.37) Be careful not to sand below the ear on the left side. Round the area that joins the body, stopping at your pencil line. (Photo 2.38)

Next pop out the nose section and taper the left side of the face so it will be lower than the nose part. (Photo 2.39) Put the nose section back in place to check your progress. If it looks correct, use a pencil to mark where this area joins the nose. (Photo 2.40) Slightly round the nose section toward this mark.

(Photo 2.41)

Now you can take all the parts off of the sanding shim. Sand the chin down about $1/8$" below the nose area. (Photo 2.42) You can tape the two pieces together with the double-sided tape. (Photo 2.43) Mark the height with pencil, then round the nose area toward the chin. (Photo 2.44) Sand both parts together, then tape it back to the shim to sand them together.

Now for some detail on the eyes. Use double-sided tape to attach the lower eyelid to the part below it. (Photo 2.45) Sand these parts together. (Some of those pieces are so small that it is easier to hold on to them this way.) Taper these parts slightly down toward the eye. (Photo 2.46) Mark the eye with a pencil. Now work on the upper eye section. Roll these parts slightly down toward the upper eyelid. (Photo 2.47) Mark the eyelid. (Photo 2.48) Round the eye lid leaving it a little thicker than the upper eye areas. Mark the upper side of the eye. I sanded the eye down a little below the pencil line with the Wonder Wheel. (Photo 2.49) Try not to have a bulging eyes: they look unnatural. (Photo 2.50) Mark the ear on the right side of the face. (Photo 2.51) Sand the ear to the same thickness as the face, then taper it toward the outside edge. (Photo 2.52)

If everything fits correctly, you can now go back and clean up the parts. Hand sand each part. I went over the face with 180-grit, followed by 220-grit. Then hand sand, or use a Wonder Wheel, to remove the sharp corners. (Photo 2.53)

Now we can add some extra detail. These are extras I like to add, however you can quit at this point. I used a wood burner to add some vertical lines on the basket, just use the pattern as a guide for placement. (Photo 2.54) I also added a highlight to the eyes by using small dowels of scrap white wood. The eyes are very small and hard to hold on to, so it may help to use some of the double-sided tape and stick the eyes to a scrap piece of wood. Carefully drill small holes, close to the size on the pattern (placement is up to you). (Photo 2.55) Use a white pencil

2.35 Sand the ear on the left side down to about $3/16$". Mark where the ear joins the face.

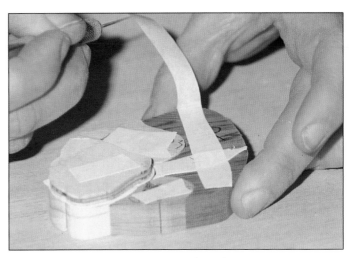

2.36 Tape all the face parts to a sanding shim.

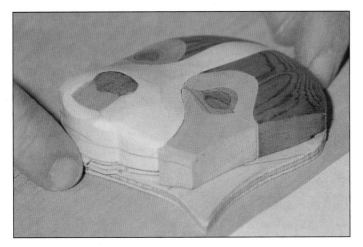

2.37 Round the head toward the top, then blend in the raised nose area. Taper the sides of the head toward the ears.

2.38 Round the area that joins the body, stopping at the pencil line that marks the height of the body on the head.

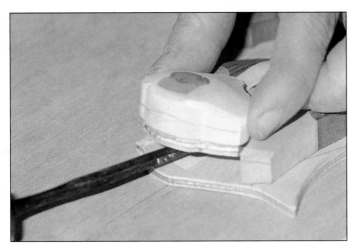

2.39 Pop out the nose section and taper the left side of the face so that it will be lower than the nose part.

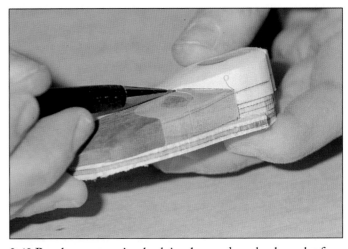

2.40 Put the nose section back in place and mark where the face joins the nose.

Project 2: Puppy in a Basket

to mark the spot to drill. **(Photo 2.56)** Cut a piece of the dowel slightly longer than needed. Put a small bead of glue in the hole and put the dowel in place. **(Photo 2.57)** When the glue dries you can sand the highlight flush with the eye. **(Photo 2.58)** You can paint this highlight. Adding this highlight always adds so much life to a project. Dust off all the pieces, and the project is ready to be finished.

STEP FOUR
Applying the Finish

After all the parts have peen sanded, checked for scratches, de-burred and dusted off, it is time to put a clear finish on the parts. Put the finish on before you glue the pieces down. It is easier to get a nice finish this way. I applied three coats, waiting at least four hours before applying each subsequent coat. I put two coats of clear satin on first, then one final coat of matte Bartley. We prefer a matte or a more satin finish as opposed to a very shiny finish. However, finishing is strictly a personal choice; it is up to you what type of finish you use. There are many types of finishes you can use. However, whatever you chose, be sure to follow the directions.

STEP FIVE
Cutting the Backing

When the finish is dry you can lay out your backing. I traced around the actual project to get an outline for the backing rather than using the pattern. Sometimes during the sanding process, pieces get altered or fit a little better with the head turned. Tracing around the actual project ensures that the backing will match the project exactly.

Note: If you are planning to mount the puppy (or any Intarsia project) to something like a jewelry box, letter holder or some other type of project, it is not necessary to make a backing. Just glue the pieces directly to the face of the project.

It helps to apply a very light coat of spray adhesive to the paper and then place the parts on top. The adhesive will keep the parts from sliding around while you trace the pelican. Cut out the pattern for the backing, then apply it to a 1/8" plywood board with spray adhesive. I've found that Baltic or Finnish birch works great for backing.

When cutting the backing stay to the inside of the pencil line. You will want the backing slightly smaller than the actual pelican.

After de-burring the backing you can put a dark stain around the edges. We did not stain the edges on these projects. Also, if there are any gaps, it helps the stain the space between the parts. Then we seal the back side with a clear acrylic spray.

STEP SIX
Gluing the Puppy Down

The puppy is now ready to glue down to the backing. Place the parts on the backing and check all the edges to make sure there no backing is exposed. If the backing is showing, you will need to mark those areas and trim them on your saw.

Pick a few key parts to lock the project in place. The bottom of the basket makes a good locking part. I use dots of wood glue, leaving space for a few dots of hot glue. Using two different types of glue is important. The hot glue sets quickly and works like a clamp. This will help anchor the project and keep the pieces from shifting as you continue.

When using hot glue, you have to move quickly and accurately before the glue sets up. Five to ten seconds is all the time you'll have before the glue sets up. After the lower basket part is set, continue gluing the rest of the puppy down. I would use the same combination of glue on all the lower basket parts, then use just the woodworkers glue on the handles and on all the puppy parts. This way you will have more time to work before the glue sets.

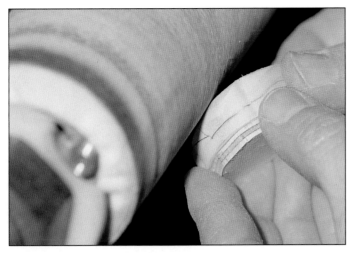

2.41 Round the nose section slightly toward this mark. Then take off the sanding shim.

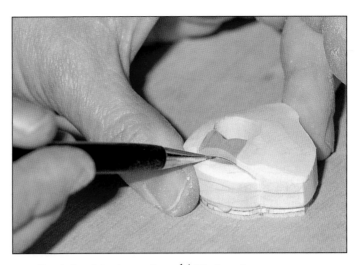

2.42 Sand the chin down about $^1/_8$" below the nose area.

2.43 Tape the two pieces together with double-sided carpet tape and mark them with a pencil.

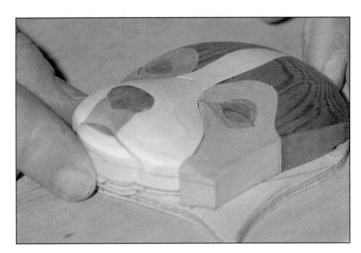

2.44 Round the nose area toward the chin.

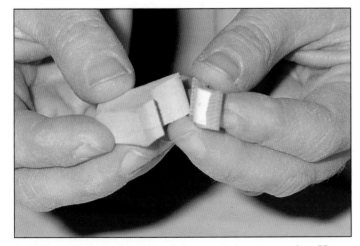

2.45 Sand the lower eyelid and the part below it together. Use double-sided tape to hold the pieces together. These pieces are so small that sanding them together will make the task easier.

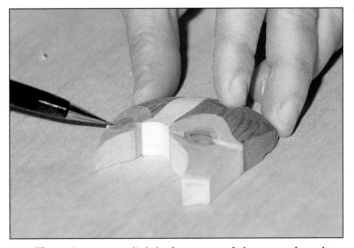

2.46 Taper these parts slightly down toward the eye and mark the eye with a pencil.

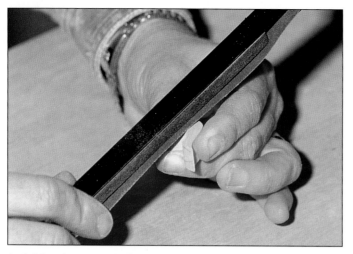

2.47 Now begin to work on the upper eye section. Roll these parts down slightly down toward the upper eyelid.

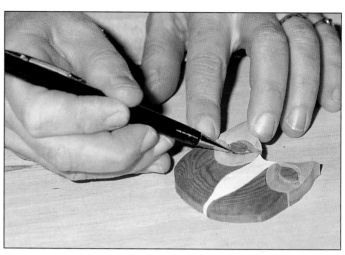

2.48 Mark the eye lid. Then round the eyelid leaving it a little thicker than the upper eye areas. Mark the upper side of the eye.

2.49 Sand the eye down a little below the pencil line.

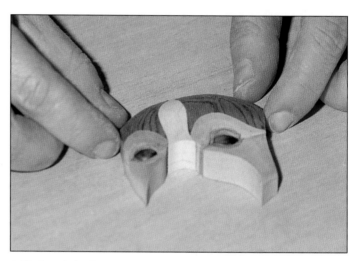

2.50 Avoid sanding below the pencil guide lines, creating unnatural-looking bulging eyes.

2.51 Mark the ear on the right side of the face.

2.52 Sand the ear to follow close to the same thickness of the face, then taper it toward the outside edge.

Intarsia Artistry

2.53 Hand sand or use a Wonder Wheel to remove the sharp corners from each part.

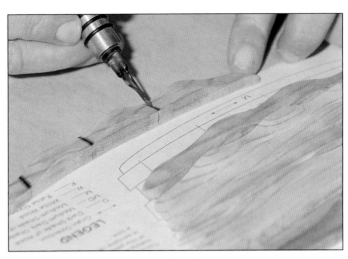

2.54 Using the pattern as a guide, add vertical lines to the basket with a woodburner. These give some additional detail and are optional.

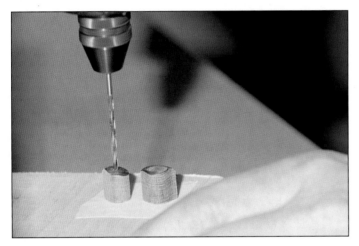

2.55 Carefully drill small holes in the eyes. Taping the eyes to a sanding shim will help to hold these small pieces in place while you drill.

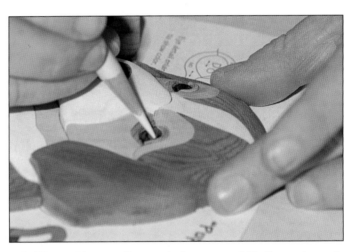

2.56 Use a white pencil to mark the spot to drill. Cut a piece of dowel slightly longer than needed.

2.57 Put a small bead of glue in the hole and put the dowel in place.

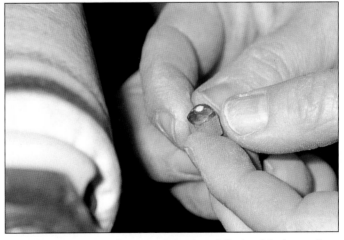

2.58 When the glue dries, sand the dowel flush with the surface of the eye. If you do not have a dowel, you can just paint the highlight.

"Puppy in a Basket"
Ways to simplify the pattern.

Do not cut the upper and lower lid area, just cut the upper and lower parts marked "M". Use a wood-burner to darken these areas if desired. The same can be applied to the dark area below the nose. Just cut the entire nose section from the "W" wood. Burn the darker area using the dashed lines as a guide.

Instead of cutting out each toe pad, use a wood-burner after it has been shaped. Follow the dashed lines as a guide.

Use a wood-burner to darken these areas.

Use a wood-burner to add these lines.

Project 3
Buffalo Indian

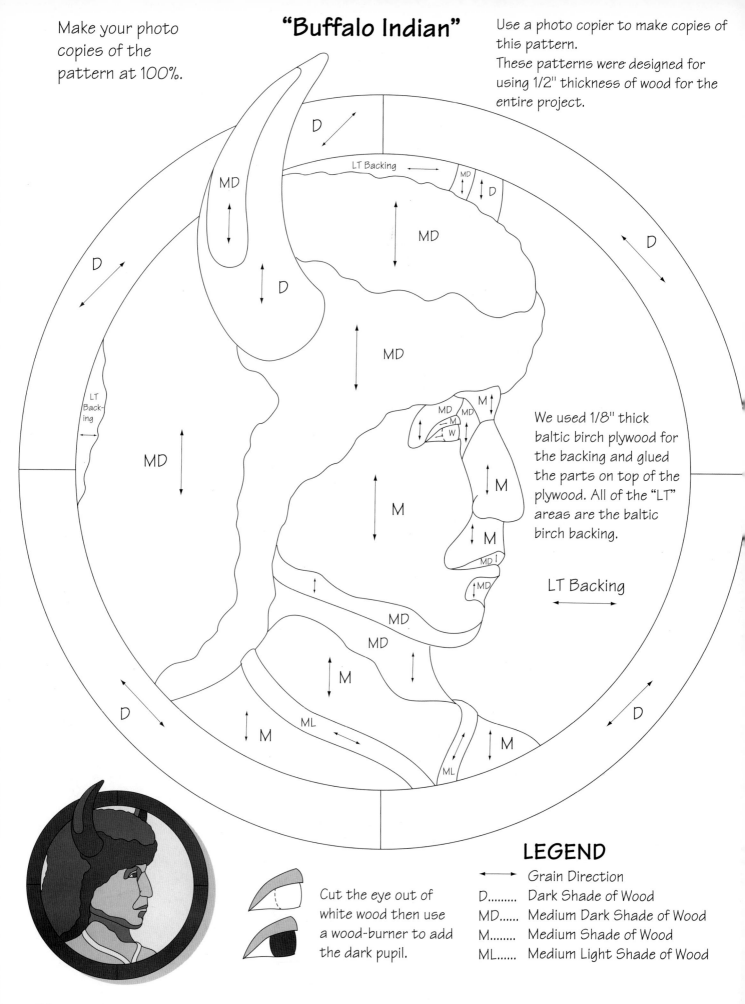

Make your photo copies of the pattern at 100%.

"Buffalo Indian"

Use a photo copier to make copies of this pattern.

These patterns were designed for using 1/2" thickness of wood for the entire project.

D

LT Backing

MD

D

MD

MD

D

D

MD

D

MD

MD

M

LT Backing

MD

MD

M

MD

M

M

M

M

MD

We used 1/8" thick baltic birch plywood for the backing and glued the parts on top of the plywood. All of the "LT" areas are the baltic birch backing.

LT Backing

LT Backing

M

M

ML

M

ML

D

D

Cut the eye out of white wood then use a wood-burner to add the dark pupil.

LEGEND

⟷ Grain Direction

D......... Dark Shade of Wood

MD...... Medium Dark Shade of Wood

M........ Medium Shade of Wood

ML...... Medium Light Shade of Wood

Intarsia Artistry

Project 3: Buffalo Indian

STEP ONE
Layout
Make at least five copies of the pattern. To layout the pattern, use the same techniques described in detail for the Pelican and the Puppy. Cut the pattern in sections and use spray adhesive to mount the pattern pieces to the wood.

STEP TWO
Sawing
For a better fit, stack cut the head dress and the horn in the forefront. I used double-sided tape to stick a medium-dark piece of wood to a dark piece. After you finish sawing the parts, swap with the appropriate pieces. You will have some waste using this technique but it does save time and the parts fit. I used a #2 scroll saw blade, which is very thin, making the wood lost in the cut, much less noticeable. After all the parts have been cut assemble the project and check how everything fits.

STEP THREE
Shaping
I cut a sanding shim to sand many parts of this project together: the head dress, the horn, the neck and the face. Sand the rim first (down to a little over $1/4$"). Then mark with a pencil where these parts join the others. Sand the neck area next, using double-sided tape to hold all the neck parts on the sanding shim. Then taper the neck down below the pencil line indicating the rim thickness. I sanded the neck down to about $1/4$" where it joins the head section. Take the neck section off the shim and mark where it joins the head, the head dress and the medium light necklace parts. Sand these necklace parts just barely above the pencil line.

Now tape all the face parts on the sanding shim. I just roughed in the parts, sanding the entire face section down about to $3/8$" and rounding the lower jaw down toward the neck section. Then take the nose

parts, the upper lip parts, the eye and the lid off of the sanding shim. Round the cheek and upper eye area toward the nose section. Put all the facial parts back in place, then mark where the cheek joins these parts. Sand the nose down to the pencil line. Next mark the eyelid and sand it just slightly thicker than the upper eye section. Mark the eye and sand it just a little below the pencil lines. Finally put all the face parts back in place, and mark where the face joins the head dress.

At this time, I sanded the horn in the background. It helps to use the double-sided tape and tape the two parts together, side to side, and sand them together as they are rather small and hard to hold on to. After sanding, mark the head dress. Tape the head dress to the sanding shim. Sand the lower area (where it looks like it goes behind the shoulder) and the back side down below the rim mark. Round the rest of it toward the outside edges. Be sure to watch out for your pencil line showing the thickness of the face. You do not want to sand the head dress below the face.

After the head dress is shaped, and while it is still taped to the sanding shim, I put some texture on it. I used a Wonder Wheel to make a "dip-like" texture. The Wonder Wheel puts a dip in the wood and slightly burns it at the same time. If you are using hard wood, it will probably burn too much. You could use some carving tools to add texture in this area. Put the head dress back in place and mark where it joins the horn. Sand the horn, tape it to the sanding shim so you can sand the two parts together. After everything is the basic shape desired, go back and clean everything up. Hand sand where needed and burn the pupil portion of the eye. Now you are ready to apply the finish. After the finish is dry, cut your backing and glue it down.

Humming Bird

"Humming Bird"

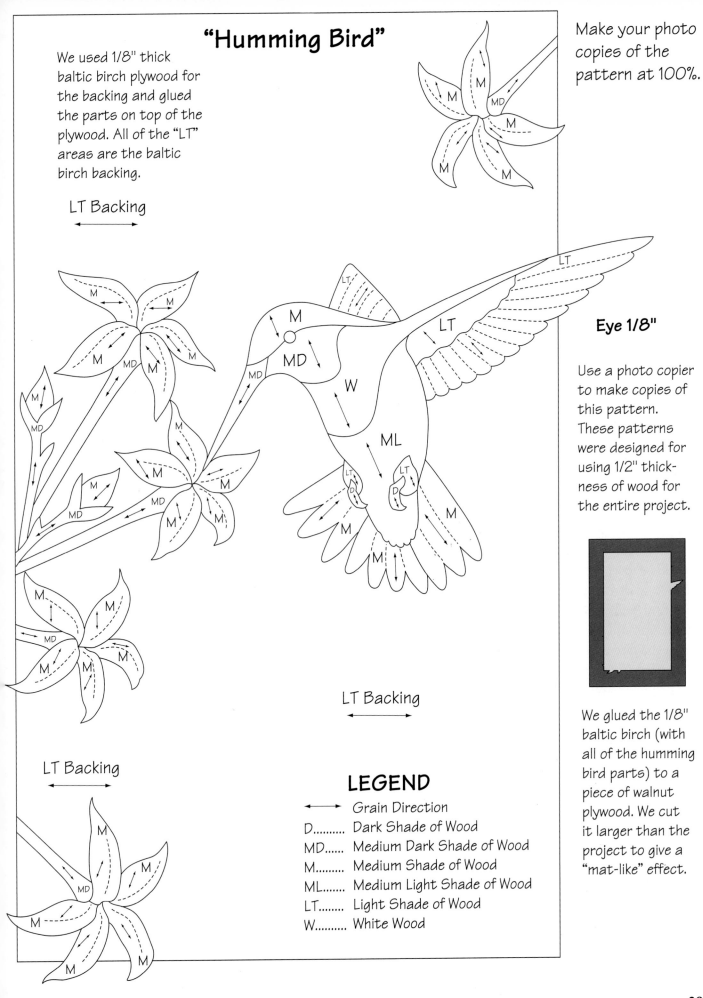

We used 1/8" thick baltic birch plywood for the backing and glued the parts on top of the plywood. All of the "LT" areas are the baltic birch backing.

LT Backing

Make your photo copies of the pattern at 100%.

Eye 1/8"

Use a photo copier to make copies of this pattern. These patterns were designed for using 1/2" thickness of wood for the entire project.

We glued the 1/8" baltic birch (with all of the humming bird parts) to a piece of walnut plywood. We cut it larger than the project to give a "mat-like" effect.

LT Backing

LT Backing

LEGEND

⟷	Grain Direction
D..........	Dark Shade of Wood
MD......	Medium Dark Shade of Wood
M.........	Medium Shade of Wood
ML.......	Medium Light Shade of Wood
LT........	Light Shade of Wood
W..........	White Wood

Project 4: Hummingbird

STEP ONE
Layout

Make at least five copies of the pattern. To layout the pattern, use the same techniques described in detail for the Pelican and the Puppy. Cut the pattern in sections and use spray adhesive to mount the pattern pieces to the wood.

STEP TWO
Sawing

We did not stack cut any of these parts. I cut the eye, but you could drill both sections if desired. After all the parts have been cut, assemble the project and check how everything fits.

STEP THREE
Shaping

I sanded some of the humming bird parts together. I cut a "sanding shim" for the bird minus the tail sections and the wing in the background. Make your sanding shim and put it aside for now. Sand the tail parts first. I sanded mine down to about $1/4$". After sanding, mark the body where the tail joins. Sand the background wing, then mark where it joins the body. Now tape all the parts, except the light leg sections and the dark feet parts, to the sanding shim. Sand the humming bird body, rounding the head area back toward the background wing. Then round the beak, blending it with the face parts. Taper the body down toward the pencil lines showing the thickness of the tail feathers. Do not sand below the tail feathers. Next take off the two light wing parts. First sand the lower wing portion. Taper it toward the body and in toward the upper wing portion. Put it back in place and mark with a pencil where it joins the upper wing section. Then sand the upper wing, tapering it toward the body and down toward the pencil line. Put it back in place and mark where it joins the body. Now sand the body down to the pencil line. This will make the wing appear to be coming from behind the bird.

Next put the leg and foot sections in place, mark them with a pencil and sand them. Leave some thickness here. You want to make the feet the thickest part, so make a stair step down to the leg sections, then make another stair step down to the body. You can put a dowel in place at this time for the eye. I round the tip of a dowel with the Wonder Wheel then put it in place and mark from the back side the length needed.

The flowers are fairly easy to sand, their small size is the only difficulty. Sand what would be the background petals first. Then work your way up the petals in the foreground. Mark where the petals join the stems and sand the stems below the pencil lines.

I used the edge of the Wonder Wheel to carve the lines in the petals and on the wings. Use the dashed lines as a guide. You can also use a wood burner, carve these areas or use the edge of a disc sander.

After everything is sanded to shape, go back and clean everything up. Hand sand where needed. Now your project is ready to be finished. After the finish is dry, cut your backing and glue the parts down. We glued this project directly to the backing. Then we glued the project to another piece of walnut plywood to act as a frame. You could cut off any of the parts that extend beyond the square area and put it in a frame. You could also make the backing larger so it all fits within a frame.

Project 5
Clown

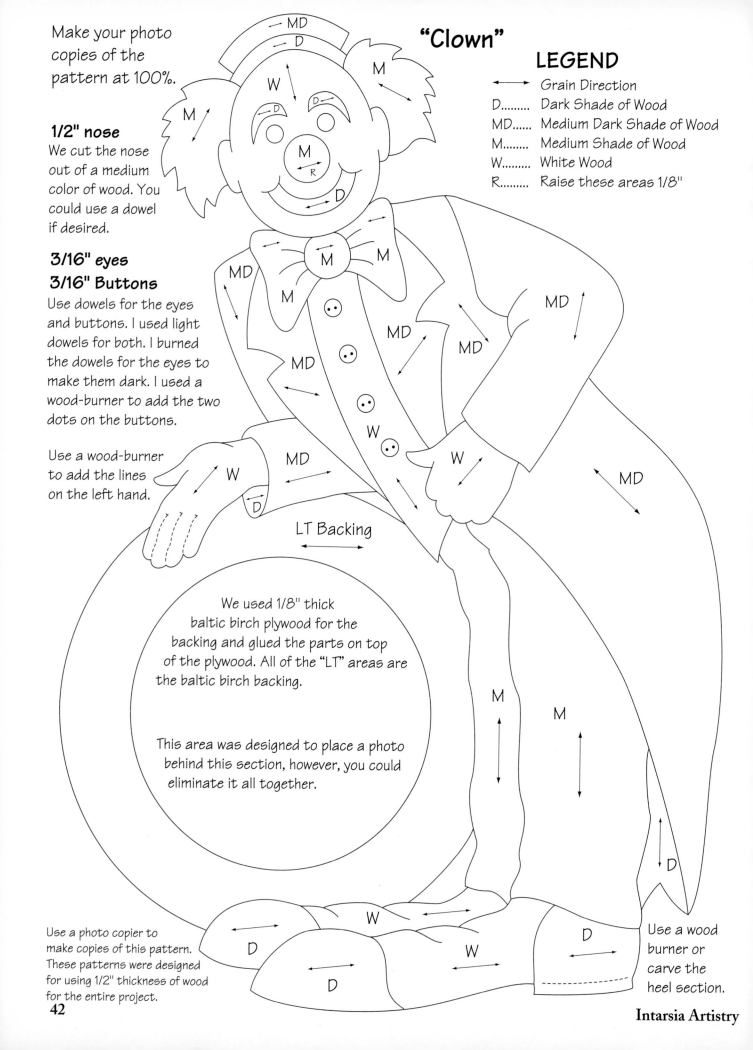

Make your photo copies of the pattern at 100%.

"Clown"

1/2" nose
We cut the nose out of a medium color of wood. You could use a dowel if desired.

3/16" eyes
3/16" Buttons
Use dowels for the eyes and buttons. I used light dowels for both. I burned the dowels for the eyes to make them dark. I used a wood-burner to add the two dots on the buttons.

Use a wood-burner to add the lines on the left hand.

LEGEND
⟷   Grain Direction
D.........   Dark Shade of Wood
MD......   Medium Dark Shade of Wood
M........   Medium Shade of Wood
W.........   White Wood
R.........   Raise these areas 1/8"

LT Backing

We used 1/8" thick baltic birch plywood for the backing and glued the parts on top of the plywood. All of the "LT" areas are the baltic birch backing.

This area was designed to place a photo behind this section, however, you could eliminate it all together.

Use a photo copier to make copies of this pattern. These patterns were designed for using 1/2" thickness of wood for the entire project.

42

Use a wood burner or carve the heel section.

Intarsia Artistry

STEP ONE
Layout

Make at least five copies of the pattern. This pattern is more complex than the others and may require additional copies of the pattern. To layout the pattern, use the same techniques described in detail for the Pelican and the Puppy. Cut the pattern in sections and use spray adhesive to mount the pattern pieces to the wood.

STEP TWO
Sawing

We did not stack cut any of these parts. I cut the hole for the nose and then drilled the eye holes. After all the parts have been cut, assemble the project and check how everything fits.

STEP THREE
Shaping

I used three sanding shims on this project: one for the face and one for each of the shoes. Always start sanding the part that is the farthest away first. In this case, the shoe in the background is a good place to start. Tape both shoes to the sanding shims, sand the background one first. I sanded mine down to about $3/16"$ then rounded it toward the outside. Leave the sanding shim in place and mark where the shoe in the background joins the shoe in the foreground. Sand this shoe down to a little over $3/8"$, then round it toward the background shoe.

Next mark where the shoes join the pants. Sand the background leg first (about $1/4"$ thick) round it toward the outside edge. Mark the next leg. Sand the foreground leg, tapering it down toward the hand. You will want the closed hand to be one of the thickest parts. Mark where the leg joins the coat and sand the coat, tapering it down toward the arm . Next mark the dark part between the coat tail and the pant leg. Sand it tapering it toward the pant leg.

Now move up to the upper coat sections. Sand the upper left part (above the left arm) down to about $1/4"$, rolling the top shoulder edge. Mark where it joins the arm. Sand the hand, tapering it down toward the

thumb side of the hand and lower the wrist section. Mark where the wrist joins the sleeve. Now sand the sleeve, rounding both the upper and the lower side, watching out for the pencil line for the shoulder area. Then sand the little dark part under the hand section. Sand it lower than the hand and the sleeve. Next sand the other shoulder section, sanding the overall thickness down to about $3/8"$ or less. Then taper it down toward the arm. Mark the adjoining parts with pencil.

Now sand the white shirt section down to about $3/8"$, mark the coat lapels. Sand the lapels, tapering them down toward the shirt and down toward the hand on the right. You will want the outside edges to be the thickest. Mark the bow tie and sand these parts. I sanded the outside bow first, tapering it down toward the center knot. Then I marked the knot and rounded it toward the pencil lines.

Now sand the hat. I stair stepped these parts. The top of the hat is the thinnest. Mark the top of the head, then sand the hair down to about $1/4"$, marking the head. Tape all the parts except the nose and the eye brows to the sanding shim. Round the face, watching the pencil lines. Do not sand below any of the pencil lines. I carved the ears down a little. Put the eyebrows in. You want these to be thicker than the face. If necessary you can raise these with an $1/8"$ shim. Mark the nose and round it like a ball. I burned the dowels for the eye to make them stand out more.

After everything is sanded to shape, go back and clean everything up. Hand sand where needed, and burn in the button holes and the lines between the fingers. Now you can apply the finish. After the finish is dry, cut your backing and glue the parts down. We glued this project directly to the backing. You can place a photo behind the circular cut-out area.

Little Angel

"Little Angel"

Make your photo copies of the pattern at 100%.

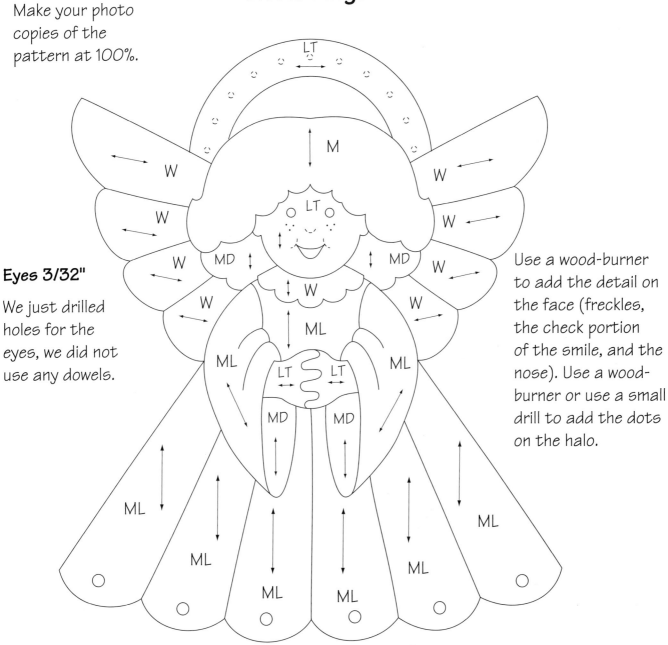

Eyes 3/32"

We just drilled holes for the eyes, we did not use any dowels.

Use a wood-burner to add the detail on the face (freckles, the check portion of the smile, and the nose). Use a wood-burner or use a small drill to add the dots on the halo.

1/8" holes on dress, use 1/8" dowels

LEGEND

↔	Grain Direction
MD......	Medium Dark Shade of Wood
M........	Medium Shade of Wood
ML......	Medium Light Shade of Wood
LT.......	Light Shade of Wood
W.........	White Wood

Use a photo copier to make copies of this pattern.

These patterns were designed for using 1/2" thickness of wood for the entire project.

Project 6: Little Angel

Make at least five copies of the pattern. To layout the pattern, use the same techniques described in detail for the Pelican and the Puppy. Cut the pattern in sections and use spray adhesive to mount the pattern pieces to the wood. Some parts, like the lower portion of the gown and wings, can be laid out on one piece of wood. As a general rule, if the wood grain and color are the same, these sections can be laid out as one piece then segmented on the saw.

We did not stack cut any of these parts. Drill the holes before sawing. After all the parts have been cut assemble the project, and check how everything fits.

Always start sanding the part that is the farthest away first. In this case the halo and the lower portion of the gown would be a good place to start. Keep working your way up to what would be the closet to the viewer. The trick is to sand parts down to get more of a "stair step" dimensional effect. Remember to use your pencil as you go and mark the adjoining parts. The "M" hair part should be the thickest part, therefore it should be sanded last.

After everything is sanded to shape, go back and clean everything up. Hand sand where needed. Burn the freckles, nose and the dots on the halo if you did not drill those. If you do not have a wood burner, you can paint the extra detail, however, it would be better to apply the finish before painting. After the finish is dry, cut your backing and glue the parts down.

Project 7: Raccoon

Make copies of the pattern. Cut the pattern in sections and use spray adhesive to mount the pattern pieces to the wood.

I used a "Manzanita" root to frame the raccoon face. With a band saw, I sliced the root to have one flat side. Then I cut the center section to inlay the raccoon face. I traced the cut-out section onto the pattern, then modified the pattern to fit the cut-out section. I tried to follow some of the natural lines in the root. If you do not have any unusual pieces of wood lying around you can use the pattern and cut these areas from different pieces of wood, as shown on the pattern.

Drill the eyes before cutting those sections. We did not stack cut any of these parts. After all the parts have been cut, assemble the project and check how everything fits. The face can be sanded together. Cut a sanding shim the same shape as the entire face. Also cut the shims for raising areas as needed. Cut the shim to raise the entire section, rather than cutting a shim for each piece.

Sand the dark area in the background first, then the raccoon body next, marking with a pencil as you go. Use double-sided tape to hold the parts to the sanding shim. Be sure to include the shim to raise the parts indicated on the pattern. Use the double-sided tape to secure the raised areas to the shim, then tape that section to the sanding shim for the entire face. With everything in place, blend the raised areas into the rest of the face. Leave the nose the thickest and taper everything back toward the body. When you feel reasonably close, take the parts off of the sanding shim.

After everything is sanded to shape, go back and clean everything up. Hand sand where needed. For extra detail use a wood burner to add more grain lines, use the dashed lines as a guide.

Now you are ready to apply the finish. After the finish is dry, trace around the project onto the backing. Cut the backing and glue the parts down.

Project 7

Raccoon

"Raccoon"

This project was inspired by Scott Leech. He made us a wonderful piece of Intarsia, which he inlaid two raccoon faces into a maple burl.

Use a photo copier to make copies of this pattern. These patterns were designed for using 1/2" thickness of wood for the entire project.

For added detail use a woodburner to add some grain lines, used the dashed lines as a guide.

Make your photo copies of the pattern at 100%.

LEGEND

→ .... Grain Direction
D......... Dark Shade of Wood
MD......... Medium Dark Shade of Wood
M......... Medium Shade of Wood
W......... White Wood
R......... Raise these areas 1/8"

I found a "Manzanita" root to make the log portion of this pattern. If you have any unusual pieces of wood or logs that you can cut up, it adds to the over all effect of this project. If none are available use the pattern above to make your own.

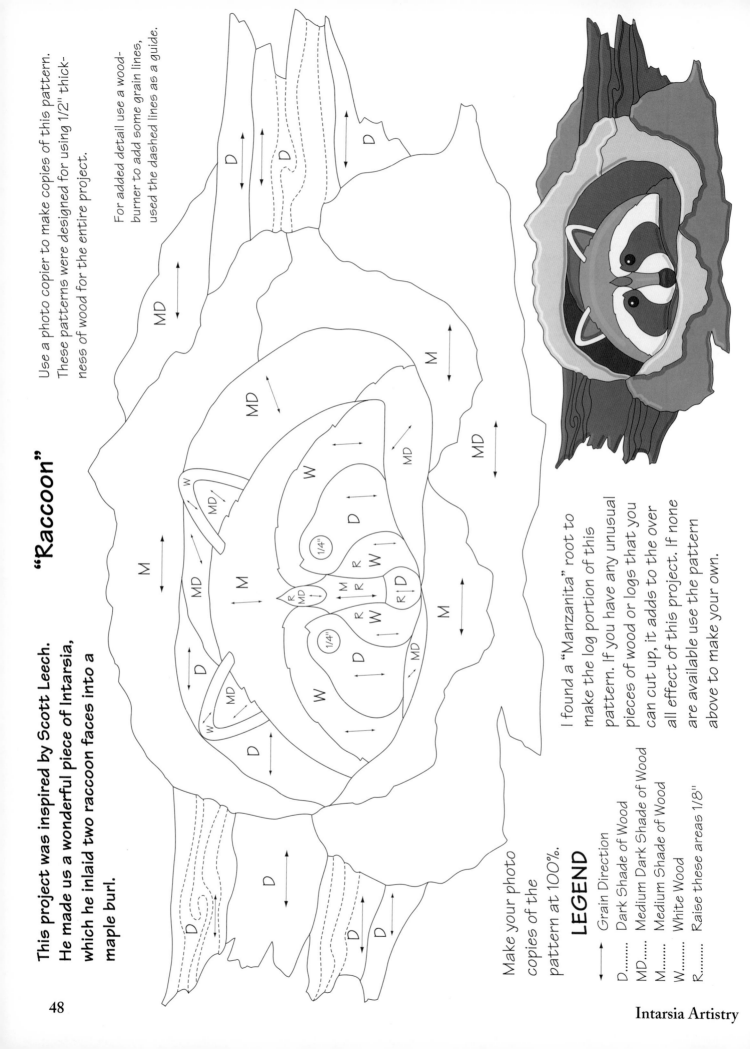

48

Hands

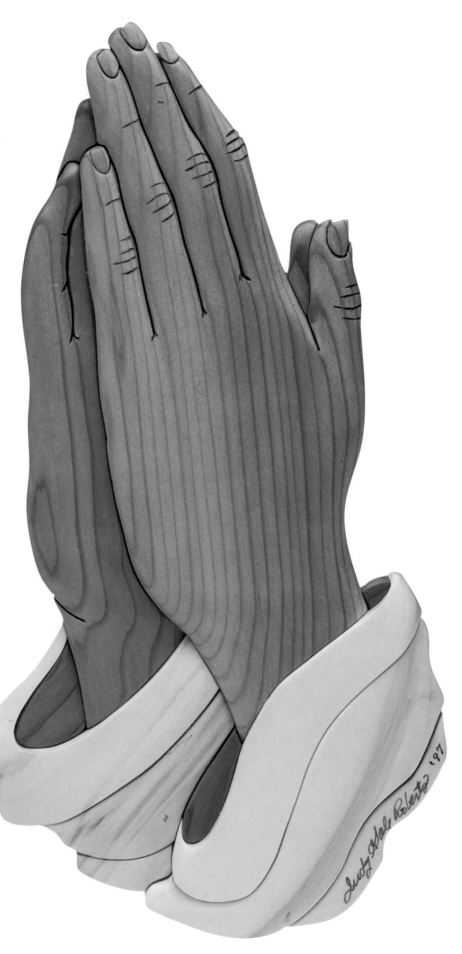

"Praying Hands"

Make your photo copies of the pattern at 100%.

LEGEND

←——→	Grain Direction
M........	Medium Shade of Wood
ML......	Medium Light Shade of Wood
LT.......	Light Shade of Wood
W.........	White Wood

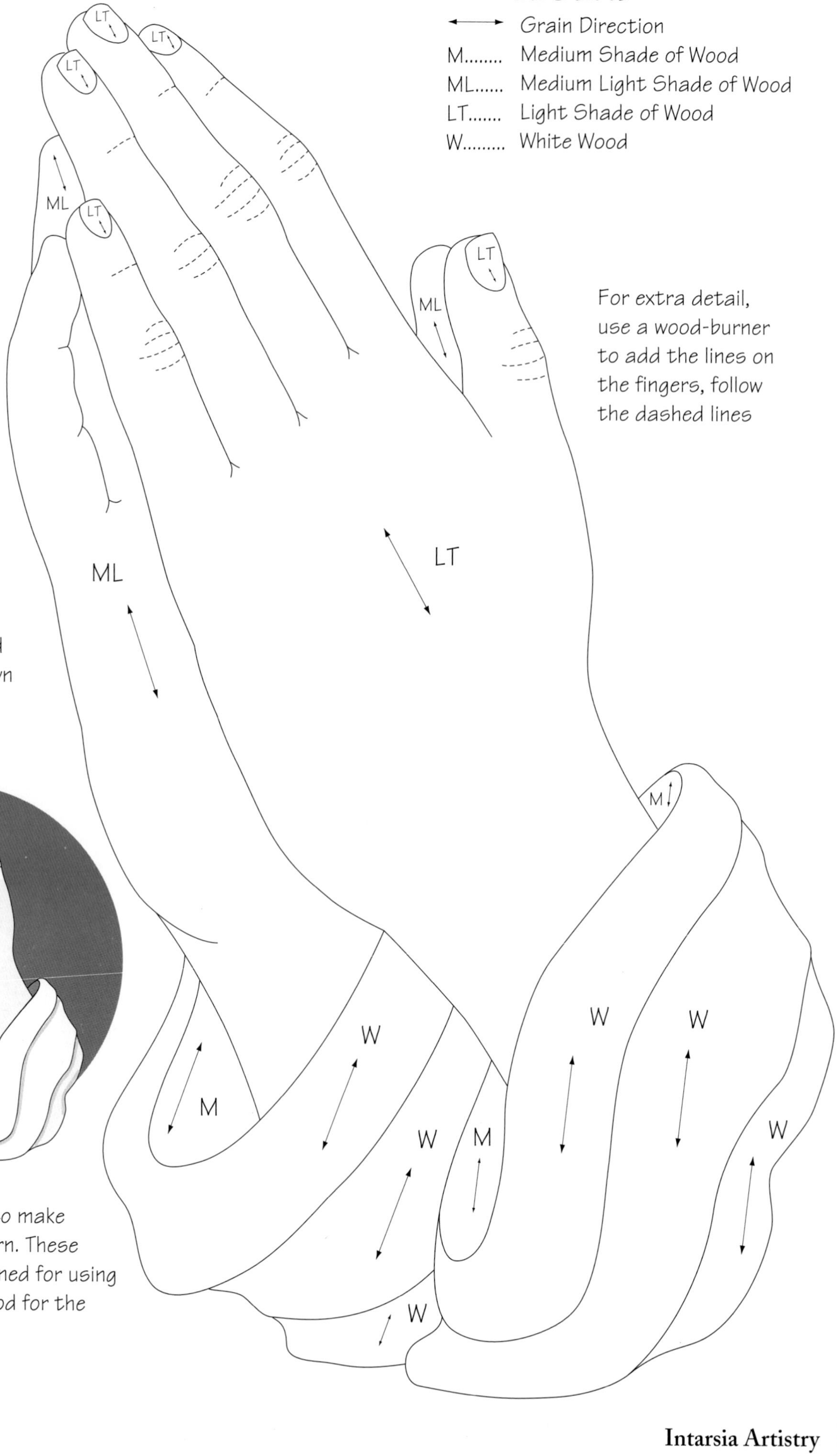

To eliminate a few pieces you could use a wood-burner to make the finger nail lines.

For extra detail, use a wood-burner to add the lines on the fingers, follow the dashed lines

This project would look great mounted on a circle, as shown below.

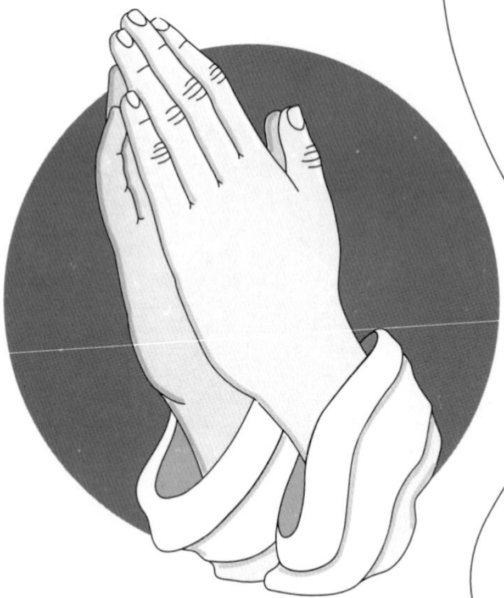

Use a photo copier to make copies of this pattern. These patterns were designed for using 1/2" thickness of wood for the entire project.

Project 8: Praying Hands

Make copies of the pattern. Cut the pattern in sections and use spray adhesive to mount the pattern pieces to the wood.

We did not stack cut any of these parts. To eliminate some of the pieces you can use a wood burner to make the finger nail lines. After all the parts have been cut, assemble the project and check how everything fits.

Sand the left background hand first, then the thumb. After sanding put the parts back and mark where they join the rest of the project. Next, sand the left hand sleeve. Mark where the sleeve joins the right hand. Sand the right hand, watching not to sand below the pencil line that shows how thick the left hand is. Then sand the right sleeve.

After everything is sanded to shape, go back and clean everything up. Hand sand where needed. Use a wood burner to add the knuckle lines in the fingers.

Now you are ready to apply the finish. After the finish is dry, trace around the project onto the backing. As mentioned on the pattern, this project would look great mounted on a circle, maybe using some dark wood to make the hands stand out. Cut the backing and the project is ready to glue down.

Project 9: Santa

Make copies of the pattern. Cut the pattern in sections and use spray adhesive to mount the pattern pieces to the wood. This would look good with some color. We used natural wood, however, you could cut medium-colored wood for suit parts and all the trimmings for the suit and the beard from white wood. Then, after shaping, use a red stain to add a little color.

We did not stack cut any of these parts. After all the parts have been cut, assemble the project and check how everything fits. We did not inlay the eyes. Just cutting the eyes gives it enough definition. Cut a shim to raise the left hand.

Sand the lower portion of the chimney first. Use a pencil to mark the adjoining parts as you go. Work your way up to the thicker parts.

After everything is sanded to shape, go back and clean everything up. Hand sand where needed.

Now you are ready to apply the finish. After the finish is dry, trace around the project onto the backing. Cut the backing and the project is ready to glue down.

Santa

Make your photo
copies of the
pattern at 100%.

We did not inlay the eyes, just cutting the eyes
gives it enough definition.

"Santa"

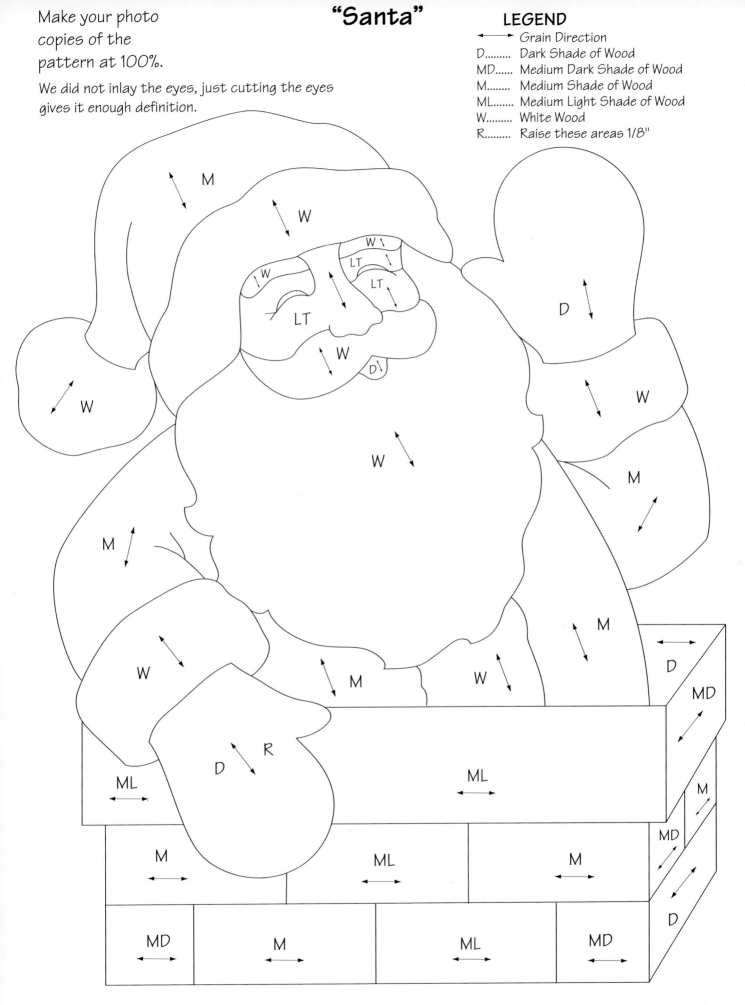

Butterfly

Make your photo copies of the pattern at 100%.

Drill 1/8" holes and use 1/8" dowels on the butterfly.

"Butterfly"

Use a photo copier to make copies of this pattern.

These patterns were designed for using 1/2" thickness of wood for the entire project.

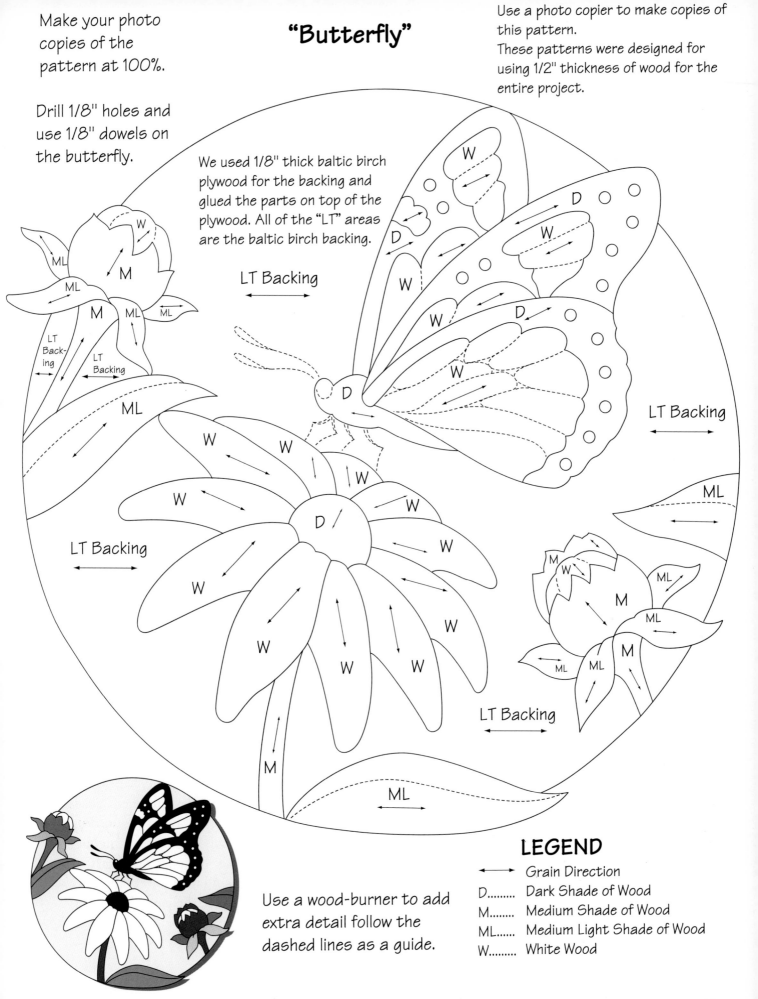

We used 1/8" thick baltic birch plywood for the backing and glued the parts on top of the plywood. All of the "LT" areas are the baltic birch backing.

LT Backing

W

W

D

D

W

D

D

W

W

W

W

LT Backing

W

M

ML

ML

M

ML

ML

M

ML

LT Back-ing

LT Backing

ML

LT Backing

W

W

W

W

W

W

D

W

W

W

W

W

M

ML

LT Backing

M

W

M

ML

M

ML

ML

ML

M

ML

LT Backing

ML

Use a wood-burner to add extra detail follow the dashed lines as a guide.

LEGEND

→ Grain Direction
D......... Dark Shade of Wood
M........ Medium Shade of Wood
ML...... Medium Light Shade of Wood
W......... White Wood

Intarsia Artistry

55

Project 10: Butterfly

Make at least five copies of the pattern. To layout the pattern, use the same techniques described in detail for the Pelican and the Puppy. Cut the pattern in sections and use spray adhesive to mount the pattern pieces to the wood. Use the pattern to make your backing, we glued the parts directly to the light backing.

We did not stack cut any of these parts. Drill the holes before sawing. After all the parts have been cut, assemble the project and check how everything fits. The butterfly wings can be sanded together. Cut a sanding shim the same shape as each wing. Use double-sided tape to hold the parts to the sanding shim. Be sure to include the small dowels when sanding, that way you can sand all the parts at one time.

Sand the back wing first, then mark with a pencil where it joins the other wing. After both wings are sanded, mark where they join the body. There are no parts touching the butterfly, so it can be sanded before the other parts. Start on the flowers next, sanding the part of the flower that is the farthest away first.

After everything is sanded to shape, go back and clean everything up. Hand sand where needed. Burn the lines on the leaves, wings, legs and antennas. If you do not have a wood burner you can paint the extra detail, however, it would be better to apply the finish before painting. Another option would be to use your saw and cut the "veining" lines for the legs and antenna, then cut the leaves and the individual segments on the wings. Now you are ready to apply the finish. After the finish is dry, glue the parts down. You may need to use your pattern as a guide for gluing.

Project 11: Lion

Make at least five copies of the pattern. This is a complex pattern and may require additional copies. To layout the pattern, use the same techniques described in detail for the Pelican and the Puppy. Cut the pattern in sections and use spray adhesive to mount the pattern pieces to the wood.

We did not stack cut any of these parts. Drill the holes for the highlight in the eyes before sawing. After all the parts have been cut, assemble the project and check how everything fits. The face can be sanded together, cut a sanding shim the same shape as the entire face. Also cut the shims for raising sections where needed. Cut the shim to raise the entire section, rather than cutting a shim for each piece.

Use double-sided tape to hold the parts to the sanding shim. Be sure to include the shim to raise the parts indicated on the pattern. For example, use the double-sided tape to secure the raised areas of the face to the shim, then tape that section to the sanding shim for the entire face. With everything in place blend the raised areas into the rest of the face. Keep the nose the thickest part and taper everything back toward the mane. Roll the upper eyelid area down toward the eye, then round the sides of the nose slightly down toward the cheeks. Also blend the "L" cheek parts down toward the "ML" sections under the eyes. Just rough in all the parts first, because this is a rather complex pattern to shape. When you feel reasonably close take the parts off of the sanding shim and mark where all the face parts join the mane. I stair stepped the mane, sanding the outer parts down the lowest and working my way up to the pencil line for the face. Sand the ears lower than the mane in front.

After everything is sanded to shape, go back and clean everything up. Hand sand where needed. Add the highlights to the eyes. Refer to the Puppy in a Basket project for details on making a highlight.

Now you are ready to apply the finish. After the finish is dry, trace around the project onto the backing. Cut the backing and glue the parts down.

Lion

"Lion"

Make your photo
copies of the
pattern at 100%.

The raised areas can be raised using
one piece of plywood, rather
than raising each piece.

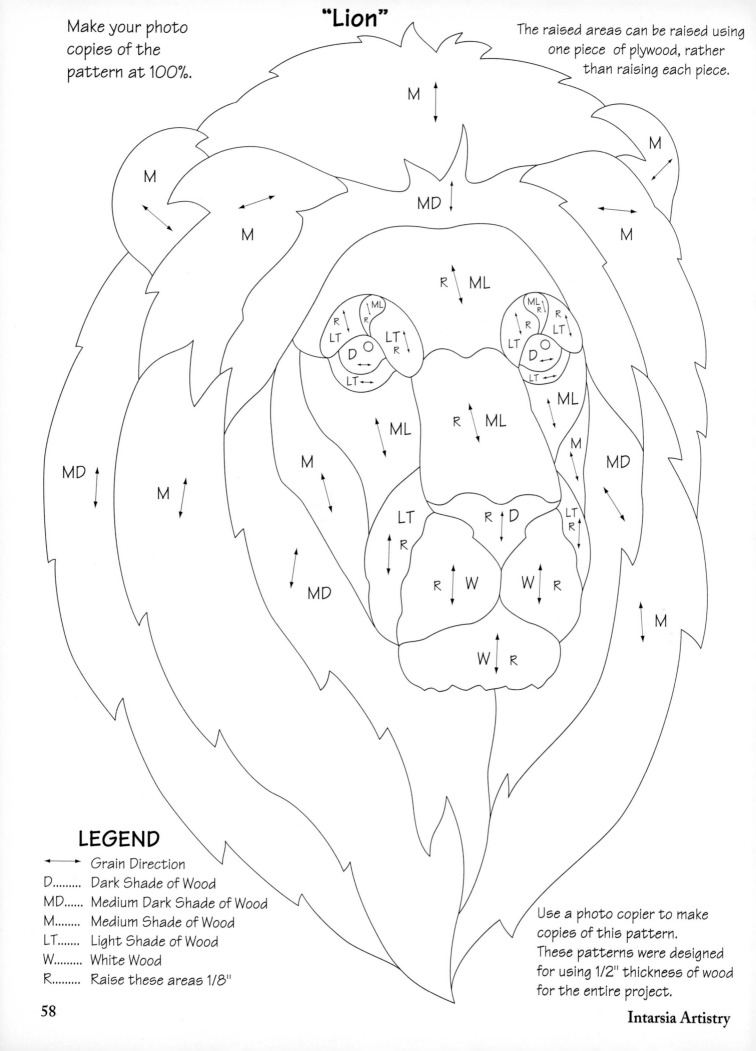

LEGEND

→ Grain Direction
D......... Dark Shade of Wood
MD...... Medium Dark Shade of Wood
M........ Medium Shade of Wood
LT....... Light Shade of Wood
W........ White Wood
R......... Raise these areas 1/8"

Use a photo copier to make
copies of this pattern.
These patterns were designed
for using 1/2" thickness of wood
for the entire project.

Intarsia Artistry

Project 12: Panda

Make at least five copies of the pattern. To layout the pattern, use the same techniques described in detail for the Pelican and the Puppy. Cut the pattern in sections and use spray adhesive to mount the pattern pieces to the wood. Use the pattern to make your backing, we glued the parts directly to the light backing.

We did not stack cut any of these parts. Drill the holes before sawing. After all the parts have been cut, assemble the project and check how everything fits. Cut a shim to raise the nose sections, as indicated on the pattern.

Remember to sand the part that would be the farthest away first. In this case, the left leg and the left ear is a good place to start. The raised nose is the last part to sand.

After everything is sanded to shape, go back and clean everything up. Hand sand where needed. Now the project is ready to be finished. After the finish is dry, glue the parts down. You may need to use your pattern as a guide for gluing.

Project 12
Panda

"Panda"

LEGEND

←——→ Grain Direction
D........ Dark Shade of Wood
M........ Medium Shade of Wood
W........ White Wood
R........ Raise these areas 1/8"

Use a photo copier to make copies of
this pattern.

These patterns were designed for
using 1/2" thickness of wood for the
entire project.

Eyes 1/8"

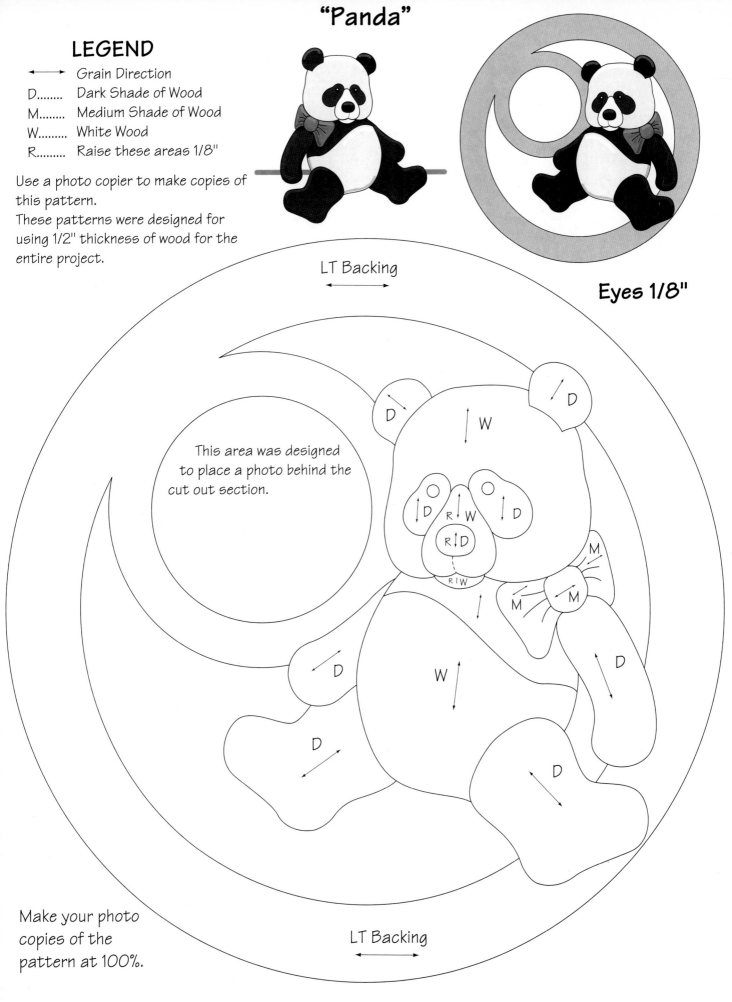

LT Backing

This area was designed
to place a photo behind the
cut out section.

LT Backing

Make your photo
copies of the
pattern at 100%.

Buyers Guide

The following hardware items may be available from your local woodworking store or from many mail-order catalog companies.
Flex Drum Sander
Intarsia Detail Sander
Wonder Wheel
12" Aspen Plate
Bartley Wiping Gel (Clear or White)
Bartley Wiping Gel (Matte)
If you have trouble locating any of the above items please contact Roberts Studio at 800-316-9010 for details on ordering direct.

If you are interested in receiving our free newsletter called the "Intarsia Times" please write to:
Roberts Studio
P.O. Box 4718
Sevierville, TN 37864-4718

Double Pneumatic Drum Sander
Sand-Rite Manufacturing Company
321 North Justine Street
Chicago, IL 60607
(312) 997-2200

THE "FINE LINE DESIGN" BOOK SERIES
SCROLL SAW • FRETWORK PATTERN BOOKS *BY JUDY GALE ROBERTS*

The "Fine Line Design" is an original idea developed by professional artist Judy Gale Roberts and craftsman Jerry Booher.

These new designs are drawn with a line so thin, that when using a #1 scroll saw blade the line will be completely removed. By using the new "Fine Line" patterns, you will be able to better control the drift error found with thick line drawings (just drifting from one side of a thick line to the other will cause problems with the overall accuracy of a design).

Especially designed for the scroll saw enthusiast who wishes to excel at their hobby or profession. This eye-catching collection of new designs offers the working crafts-person or artist timesaving, professionally executed, ready to use patterns.

The Ornament above is a sample pattern from Design Book #8 "Christmas". (the areas marked with a "X" are cut out).

FINE LINE DESIGN BOOKS AVAILABLE

DESIGN BOOK #1
A GENERAL SUBJECT BOOK OF PATTERNS, FROM COWS TO PELICANS. $14.95

DESIGN BOOK #2
"WESTERN AND SOUTHWESTERN" PATTERNS OF COWBOYS, INDIANS, AND EVERY-THING IN BETWEEN. $16.95

DESIGN BOOK #3
"THE GREAT OUTDOORS" PATTERNS OF OUTDOOR SCENES FROM FISHING TO HOT AIR BALLOONS. $14.95

DESIGN BOOK #4
"SPORTS" PATTERNS, FROM BASEBALL TO FOOTBALL. $14.95

DESIGN BOOK #5
"HEARTLAND" PATTERNS OF RURAL AMERICA, INCLUDING FARMS TO BARNS. $14.95

DESIGN BOOK #6
"PETS AND PEOPLE" PATTERNS OF CATS TO DOGS AND MANY OTHER PETS. $14.95

DESIGN BOOK #7
"CIRCUS AND CLOWNS" PATTERNS OF CLOWNS, CIRCUS ANIMALS AND A WONDERFUL CIRCUS TRAIN. $14.95

DESIGN BOOK #8
"CHRISTMAS" PATTERNS OF ALL THE TRADITIONAL CHRISTMAS ITEMS. $14.95

INTARSIA PATTERNS available from JUDY GALE ROBERTS • Roberts Studio

P.O. BOX 4718 • SEVIERVILLE, TN 37864 • 1 (800) 316-9010 • (423) 428-8875 • FAX (423) 428-7870

FOR A MORE DETAILED DESCRIPTION WITH PICTURES OF THE FOLLOWING PATTERNS,
PLEASE WRITE OR CALL THE ABOVE ADDRESS AND ASK FOR A COPY OF THE "INTARSIA TIMES".

PANDA	MANATEE	GIRAFFE	CAT ON SHELF
TOUCAN	POLAR BEAR	COYOTE	FOOTBALL PLAYER
RACCOON	TIGER	STILL POTTERY	WOOD DUCK
CAT IN BAG	ELEPHANT	WOLF	GERMAN SHEPHERD
SEASCAPE	BLACK RHINO	OL' BLUE	BLACK GEAR
ROSE	SANTA	FAWN AND DOE	MARE & FOAL
CAT WITH YARN	WREATH	WHITE TAIL DEER	GREVY'S ZEBRA
KOALA BEARS	DOLPHIN	CHRISTMAS SIGN	PRAYING HANDS
BIG FOOT CLOWN	PENGUINS	ANGEL	KITTEN AND BEAR
CLOWN IN WINDOW	DOG	ASIAN LION	PRONGHORN
CLOWN WITH DAISIES	U S A EAGLE	BARN	CROSS WITH DOVE
BUCK DEER	COW	GOLFER	LONGHORN
HORSE	BEARS	BATTER UP	SQUIRREL
BUTTERFLY AND ORCA	SWAN	CASTLE	UNICORN
OH HOOT WEST	SAIL BOAT	ROOSTER WEATHER VEIN	CANADIAN GANDER
MOUSE	ARIZONA	BALD EAGLE	CANADIAN GOOSE
CHRISTMAS STOCKINGS	UP CARROUSEL	ELK	HOWLING WOLF
PELICAN	DOWN CARROUSEL	HUMMING BIRD	INDIAN FACE
HOBO CLOWN	CAMEL	COVERED BRIDGE	CHRISTMAS CANDLES
FLAMINGOS	ROSE BUD	CHRISTMAS STOCKINGS #2	BIG HORN
STILL LIFE	BARN OWL	CARDINALS	COTTON TAIL
LIGHT HOUSE	WABBIT	WOMAN GOLFER	ST. FRANCIS
BALLOON	TROPICAL FISH	FRUIT STILL LIFE	CARIBOU
DUCK	ANTIQUE SANTA	COWBOY	HUNTIN' BUDDIES
PIG IN A BLANKET	CHRISTMAS ORNAMENTS	PUP WITH DECOY	FEATHERED FRIENDS
BAG LADY	OH HOOT HAWAIIAN	RING NECK PHEASANT	MOM'S KITCHEN
CURIOUS COON	ROCKY TOP	RED FOX	WHITE PELICAN
BASS	CALLAS FLOWER	SNOWMAN &CHICKADEE	GRANDPA'S ANGEL
CAT IN A CHAIR	FLORIDA PANTHER	NOAH'S ARK	NATURE BOY
BOG BUDDIES	MOOSE	SUN FLOWER WELCOME	CARDINAL & DOGWOOD

**THE PATTERNS ABOVE ARE PRINTED FULL SIZE ON 17 1/2" x 23" TRANSPARENT TRACING PAPER,
EACH PATTERN COMES WITH A 8" x 10" BLACK AND WHITE PRINT OF THE FINISHED PROJECT.
THE PATTERNS ABOVE SELL FOR $6.95 EACH OR 3 FOR $18.95 PLUS $2.75 SHIPPING**

EAGLE	WOODLAND TRAIL	SEA GULL PILING	INDIAN WOMAN
CLOUD NINE	EAGLE LANDING	BUFFALO	MACAW PARADISE
LAST SUPPER	INDIAN	ON A LIMB COON	ALLIGATOR DREAMS
	OWL		

**THE PATTERNS ABOVE ARE PRINTED FULL SIZE ON 25" x 38" TRANSPARENT TRACING PAPER,
EACH PATTERN COMES WITH A 8" x 10" BLACK AND WHITE PRINT OF THE FINISHED PROJECT.
THE LARGER SIZE PATTERNS ABOVE SELL FOR $7.95 EACH OR 3 FOR $21.95**

Buy one or all of the patterns available for just one shipping charge of $2.75.

ALSO AVAILABLE;

THREE POSTER PATTERN SETS, "THE HIDDEN FOREST", "NEW SHOES", AND "AFRICAN ADVENTURE EACH SET COMES WITH A PATTERN AND A 19" x 25 " FULL COLOR POSTER SUITABLE FOR FRAMING. $24.95 EACH PLUS 2.75 SHIPPING.

"FAMILY AFFAIR" COMES WITH 13" X 19" COLOR POSTER AND THE FINISHED FRAME SIZE IS 32.5" X 38". $19.95 EACH PLUS 2.75 SHIPPING.

A 90 MINUTE INTARSIA INSTRUCTIONAL VIDEO WHICH COVERS A BEGINNER LEVEL PATTERN FROM START TO FINISH.

NEW WOODWORKING TITLES

Available at your favorite book supplier!

**MAKING TOYS:
HEIRLOOM CARS AND
TRUCKS TO BUILD**
*by Sam Martin
and Roger Schroeder*
1-56523-079-5
$14.95

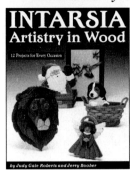

**INTARSIA:
ARTISTRY IN WOOD**
by Judy Gale Roberts

1-56523-096-5
$14.95

**CHRISTMAS SCROLL SAW
PATTERNS AND DESIGNS**
by Tom Zieg

1-56523-093-0
$12.95

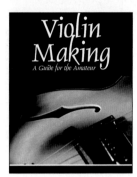

**VIOLIN MAKING
FOR THE AMATEUR**
by Bruce Ossman

1-56523-091-4
$14.95

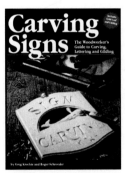

**CARVING SIGNS:
THE WOODWORKERS
GUIDE TO LETTERING,
CARVING AND GILDING**
*by Greg Krochta
and Roger Schroeder*
1-56523-078-7
$24.95 (August)

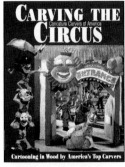

**CARVING THE CCA
CIRCUS - CARTOONING
IN WOOD**
by America's Top Carvers

1-56523-094-9
$19.95

**RELIEF CARVING
TREASURY**
by Bill Judt

1-56523-097-3
$14.95

**CARVING TROPHY
DEER AND ELK**
by Todd Swaim

1-56523-089-2
$19.95

CARVING SPOONS
by Shirley Adler

1-56523-092-2
$14.95

**REALISTIC DUCK CARVING-
A STEP-BY-STEP
ILLUSTRATED MANUAL**
by Alfred Ponte

1-56523-086-8
$9.95

**COLLAPSIBLE BASKET
PATTERNS - OVER 100
DESIGNS FOR SCROLL
SAW/BANDSAW**
by Rick Longabaugh
1-56523-087-6
$12.95

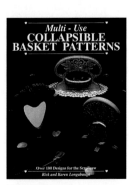

**MULTI-USE COLLAPSIBLE
BASKET PATTERNS -
OVER 100 DESIGNS/
SCROLL SAW**
by Rick Longabaugh
1-56523-088-4
$12.95

**Fox Chapel Publishing Co., Inc. • 1970 Broad Street • East Petersburg, PA 17520
1-800-457-9112 • 717-560-4702 Fax**

Scroll Saw Toys & Vehicles
By Stan Graves

Easily create contemporary toys using common materials.
• Sturdy, practical patterns
• Full color guide
• 10 patterns

$12.95
56 pages, 8.5x11, soft cover
ISBN# 1-56523-115-5

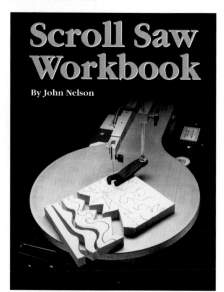

Scroll Saw Workbook
By John Nelson

This is the most practical book for learning how to use your scroll saw to make useful projects.

Veteran scroller John Nelson, drawing on 20 years of experience, has distilled down everything you need to know into 25 easy to read chapters. With accompanying patterns and illustrations, you'll quickly learn the skills needed to turn out top quality projects.

If you've been looking forward to making the most of your time spent at the scroll saw - this book is for you!

$14.95
96 pages, 8.5x11, soft cover
ISBN# 1-56523-117-1

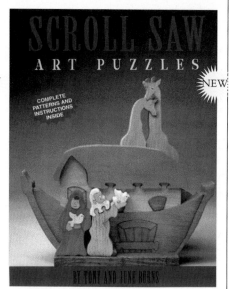

Scroll Saw Art Puzzles
By Tony and June Burns

Everyone loves a good puzzle, and with the help of this book you'll soon be scrolling delightful puzzles to brighten someone's day! Each puzzle is cut from 1 inch wood and has several interlocking cuts. When finished, the puzzles stand upright for all to admire.

Thirty-two patterns for creative projects are provided, including a fox family, a giraffe pair and Noah's ark. These puzzles-cute, classical and whimsical-will be popular for gifts or to sell.

$14.95
80 pages, 8.5x11, soft cover
ISBN# 1-56523-116-3

Scroll Saw Relief
By Marilyn Carmin

Turn your favorite fretwork pattern into something special with the techniques found in this book. First, review your basic fretwork knowledge with exercises and patterns to hone your skills. Then move on to learning scroll saw relief techniques.

You'll find helpful tips, techniques and patterns for relief scrolling and relief/fret combination scrolling. Your resulting masterpieces will showcase beautiful scroll saw work and layers of relief.

$14.95
120 pages, 8.5x11, soft cover
ISBN# 1-56523-107-4

Scroll Saw Christmas Ornaments
By Tom Zieg

Ready to try something new?
• More than 200 ornament patterns
• Wood, brass & copper designs
• Inexpensive yet beautiful gift ideas

$9.95
64 pages, 8.5x11, soft cover
ISBN# 11-56523-123-6

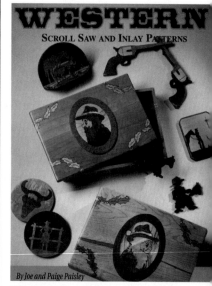

Western Scroll Saw and Inlay Projects
By Joe and Paige Paisley

The Paisleys share two tremendous talents in this brand new book for scrollers. First you'll learn the simple techniques for creating beautiful inlays on your scroll saw. With their instructions, you'll crea boxes, portraits, ornaments and even kitchen cabine doors that feature incredibly beautiful inlays.

Secondly, Joe and Paige offer their incredible collec tion of designs and patterns for Western themed scroll saw projects. Cowboy, cowgirl, Native American and animal designs are among the popula patterns you'll find in this book.

$14.95
100 pages, 8.5x11, soft cover
ISBN# 11-56523-118-X

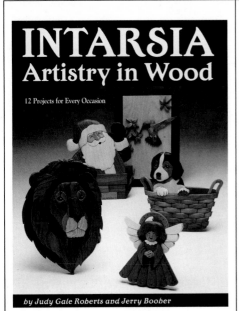

INTARSIA
Artistry in Wood

12 Projects for Every Occasion

by Judy Gale Roberts and Jerry Boober

**Intarsia-Artistry in Wood:
12 Projects for Every Occasion**
By Judy Gale Roberts and Jerry Booher

- 12 all-new, beautiful projects
- Complete instructions, patterns & color photographs
- Use the natural color and grain of the wood-no painting or staining required!

$14.95
62 pages, 8.5x11, soft cover
ISBN# 1-56523-096-5

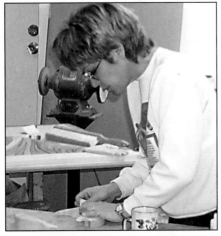

Meet Judy Gale Roberts

Raised by supportive parents in an artistic environment, Judy Gale Roberts had no problems deciding the direction of her career. Choosing an apprenticeship with her father over a formal art school education, she started working with many different media before focusing on wood. In the mid-1980s, she met and began working with Jerry Booher, a general machinist and toolmaker. Combining his mechanical ability with her artistic skills, they quickly developed a successful partnership. To this day they are still dedicated to increasing the knowledge and popularity of intarsia-artistry in wood.

---

4 Easy Ways To Order!

1 Order by Phone:
**1-800-457-9112
or 717-560-4703 (PA)**
Customer Service Representatives are ready to assist you Monday - Friday 9:00 AM-5:00 PM (EST) Please have your Visa, Mastercard or Discover account number ready. Voice Mail is available 24 hours a day.

2 Order by Fax:
717-560-4702
Just write your order and credit card number with expiration date on a piece of paper & fax it to us anytime!

3 Order by Mail:
Send your order with check or money order with shipping (see rates below) included to:
Fox Books
1970 Broad Street NW.
East Petersburg, PA 17520
PLEASE DO NOT SEND CASH!

4 Order via Email/Online:
Email your order to:
sales@carvingworld.com
Order your favorite titles on-line at:
www.carvingworld.com

Don't Forget!
- *Make all checks/money orders payable to: Fox Chapel Publishing.*
- *Please pay in US FUNDS only (available at any bank or post office)*
- *PA residents please add 6% sales tax.*

Shipping
Most orders are shipped within 24 hours. If you need your books right away, please ask about overnight service when you call.

Order Subtotal	Shipping Cost	
	USA	CANADA
$30 and under	$3	$5
$30.01 to $75	$4	$6
Over $75	$5	$8
FOREIGN orders will be billed the actual shipping cost.		

Easy To Make
INLAY WOOD PROJECTS
Intarsia
Complete Patterns and Techniques-3rd Edition

By Judy Gale Roberts and Jerry Booher

**Easy To Make Inlay Wood Projects:
Intarsia-3rd Edition**
By Judy Gale Roberts and Jerry Booher

The best book for beginning Intarsia!
- Easy-to-follow instructions
- 12 ready-to-use patterns for beginner to advanced projects
- Step-by-step demonstration
- Tips on technique

$19.95
147 pages, 8.5x11,
soft cover
ISBN# 1-56523-055-8

Sign up for Scroll Saw School!

Judy Gale Roberts and husband Jerry Booher have announced their plans for the opening of an Intarsia school at the Mountain top studio in Sevierville, Tennessee. Sevierville is located only five miles from Pigeon Forge, which has attractions ranging from Country Western theaters to the Dollywood theme park.

The focus will be on small, hands-on classes for beginner to advanced Intarsia enthusiasts. They also hope have scroll saw classes led by well-known instructors.

Jerry says "This was our plan all along when we decided to move from Texas to Tennessee. We have given seminars before but they involved so much travel for us that we were just totally worn out. We think that this area, with Dollywood and other attractions, will provide entertainment opportunities for the whole family while one or both parents attend classes."

The opening is scheduled for April, 2000. More information will be published in their Intarsia Times fall newsletter. For a free copy of the newsletter, please call 1-800-316-9010.

Wood Carving
ILLUSTRATED
"Every Carver's How-To Magazine"